THE BRIGHT FIELD

The Bright Field

AN ANTHOLOGY OF CONTEMPORARY
POETRY FROM WALES

Edited by Meic Stephens

CARCANET

First published in 1991 by
Carcanet Press Limited
208-212 Corn Exchange Buildings
Manchester M4 3BQ

British Library Cataloguing in Publication Data
    The bright field: an anthology of contemporary poetry from Wales
    1. Poetry in English. Welsh writers 1945 – anthologies
    I. Stephens, Meic, *1938-*
    821.91408

    ISBN 0 85635 907 6

The publisher acknowledges the financial assistance
of the Welsh Arts Council

Set in 10pt Palatino by Bryan Williamson, Darwen
Printed and bound in England by SRP Ltd, Exeter

Contents

BRYAN ASPDEN   Born in Blackburn, Lancs, in 1933. Read English at Durham University. He has worked as a journalist and teacher in England and Spain and is now a local government officer in Gwynedd. Married with two children, he learned Welsh after moving to Wales in 1965 and writes in the language. With his first selection of poems, *News of the Changes* (1984), he won the Welsh Arts Council's New Poets Competition and has since published another volume, *Blind Man's Meal* (1988).

JOHN BARNIE   Born in Abergavenny, Gwent, in 1941. Educated at Birmingham University, he taught for thirteen years at the University of Copenhagen before returning to Wales in 1982. Since 1985 he has worked as co-editor of the magazine *Planet* and lives near Aberystwyth. He has published three collections of poetry, *Borderland* (1984), *Lightning Country* (1987) and *Clay* (1989), as well as a volume of essays, *The King of Ashes* (1989), which won a Welsh Arts Council Prize in 1990.

DUNCAN BUSH   Born in Cardiff in 1946, educated at Warwick University and Wadham College, Oxford. He lives at Penycae in the Swansea Valley, and lectures in Cultural Studies at Gwent College of Higher Education. He has published four volumes of poetry: *Nostos* (1980), *Aquarium* (1983) and *Salt* (1985), both of which won Welsh Arts Council prizes, and *The Genre of Silence* (1988).

GILLIAN CLARKE   Born in Cardiff in 1937, read English at the University College in the city. For many years a full-time writer and teacher in creative writing, she lives now at Talgarreg in Dyfed. She was the editor of *The Anglo-Welsh Review* from 1976 to 1984. Her verse has been collected in three volumes: *The Sundial* (1978), *Letter from a Far Country* (1982) and *Letting in the Rumour* (1989); her *Selected Poems* were published in 1985.

TONY CURTIS   Born at Carmarthen in 1946 and educated at University College, Swansea, and Goddard College, Vermont, Tony Curtis is Senior Lecturer in English at the Polytechnic of Wales. He has published four collections of poetry: *Album* (1974), *Preparations* (1980), *Letting Go* (1983) and *The Last Candles* (1989); a volume of his *Selected Poems* appeared in 1986. Among the books he has edited are *The Art of Seamus Heaney* (1982), *Wales: the Imagined Nation* (1986) and two anthologies of verse about Pembrokeshire and Snowdonia. He has also contributed a monograph on Dannie Abse to the *Writers of Wales* series (1985). In 1984 he won the National Poetry Competition organized by the Poetry Society and BBC Radio 3.

JOHN DAVIES   Born at Cymmer Afan, Glamorgan, in 1944, and educated at the University College of Wales, Aberystwyth; he teaches English at Prestatyn, Clwyd. He has published five volumes of verse: *Strangers* (1974), *Spring in a Small Town* (1979), *At the Edge of Town* (1981), *The Silence in the Park* (1982) and *The Visitor's Book* (1985). With Mike Jenkins, he edited the anthology *The Valleys* (1984).

CHRISTINE EVANS   Born in West Yorkshire in 1943, and educated at the University of Exeter, she has lived in Pen Llŷn, Gwynedd, since 1967 and teaches English at Pwllheli, her father's birthplace. Her three collections of poetry are *Looking Inland* (1983), *Falling Back* (1985) and *Cometary Phases* (1989); with the last she won a Welsh Arts Council Prize in 1990.

PETER FINCH   Born in Cardiff in 1947 and educated at the Glamorgan College of Technology. He worked in local government before his appointment as Manager of the Welsh Arts Council's bookshop at Oriel, Cardiff, in 1973. He is the author of some twenty volumes of verse, including *The End of the Vision* (1971) and *Some Music and a Little War* (1984); his *Selected Poems* appeared in 1987. His short stories have been collected under the title *Between 35 and 42* (1982). The founder of the magazine *Second Aeon* in 1966, he was its editor until it ceased publication in 1974.

CATHERINE FISHER   Born in Newport in 1956, she still lives in her home-town, where she is a teacher; she was educated at the Gwent College of Further Education. Her first volume of poetry, *Immrama* (1988), won a Welsh Arts Council Prize and she won the Cardiff Literature Festival Poetry Competition in 1989. She is also the author of *The Conjuror's Game* (1990), a novel for children.

STEVE GRIFFITHS   Born on Anglesey in 1949. He has lived in London since 1970, where he co-ordinates Islington Council's programme against poverty. His three collections of poetry are *Anglesey Material* (1980), *Civilised Airs* (1984) and *Uncontrollable Fields* (1990).

PAUL GROVES   Born in 1947, brought up at The Narth, a hamlet between Monmouth and Chepstow, and educated at Caerleon College of Education. Formerly a teacher, he has recently been working on a novel and lives in Coleford, Glos. His verse has been published under the title *Academe* (1988).

DOUGLAS HOUSTON   Born in Cardiff in 1947, brought up in Glasgow and educated at the University of Hull. He returned to Wales in 1981 and now lives as a writer in Cwm Ystwyth, Dyfed. His first book of poems is *With the Offal Eaters* (1986).

MIKE JENKINS   Born in Aberystwyth in 1953 and educated at the University College in the town. He is a teacher in Merthyr Tydfil and the editor of the magazine *Poetry Wales*. Four collections of his verse have been published: *The Common Land* (1981), *Empire of Smoke* (1983), *Invisible Times* (1986) and *A Dissident Voice* (1990).

NIGEL JENKINS   Born in Gower in 1949. On leaving school he worked for four years as a newspaper reporter in England before studying literature and film at the University of Essex. He returned to Wales in 1976 and has lived since then as a writer in Swansea. He shared the Welsh Arts Council's Young Poet's Prize with Tony Curtis and Duncan Bush in 1974. Among his collections of poetry are *Song and Dance* (1981) and *Practical Dreams* (1983); a volume of his selected poems, *Acts of Union*, appeared in 1990. His play *Strike a Light!* was performed in 1985 and he has written about John Tripp in the *Writers of Wales* series.

HUW JONES   Born in 1955, brought up in Welshpool, Powys. He graduated in Theology at the University College of Wales, Aberystwyth. He was until recently a part-time tutor, teaching Welsh to adults with the Extra-Mural Department of the University College of North Wales, Bangor, but is now teaching in Botswana. His verse has been published in the volume *A Small Field* (1985).

STEPHEN KNIGHT   Born in Swansea in 1960, read English at Oxford. He has worked as a writer-in-residence in West Glamorgan and as a theatre-director in Leatherhead and Swansea. A selection of his poems appeared in *Poetry Introduction 6* (1985).

HILARY LLEWELLYN-WILLIAMS   Born in Kent in 1951, of partly Welsh parentage, took a degree in English and Theology at Southampton University. She settled in Wales in 1982 and now lives in Llanelli. In 1971 she won the Stroud Festival Guinness Poetry Competition and the Cardiff Poetry Competition in 1987. Her first volume of poetry, *The Tree Calendar* (1987), won a Welsh Arts Council Prize and her second collection, *Book of Shadows*, appeared in 1990.

CHRISTOPHER MEREDITH   Born in Tredegar, Monmouth-shire, in 1954 and educated at the University Colleges of Aberystwyth and Swansea. He once worked in a steel plant but is now a teacher in Brecon; he is a Welsh-speaker. He has published two volumes of verse, *This* (1984) and *Snaring Heaven* (1990), and a novel *Shifts* (1988), which won a Welsh Arts Council Prize.

ROBERT MINHINNICK   Born in Neath in 1952, educated at the University Colleges of Aberystwyth and Cardiff. He has worked in industry, for the Post Office and as manager of an enviromental project on the Glamorgan Heritage Coast; he is an active member of Friends of the Earth and lives in Porth-cawl. His five collections of poetry are *A Thread in the Maze* (1978), *Native Ground* (1979), *Life Sentences* (1983), *The Dinosaur Park* (1985) and *The Looters* (1989).

SHEENAGH PUGH   Born in Birmingham in 1950, of partly
Welsh parentage, and has lived in Wales since 1971. She read
Russian and German at Bristol University and then worked in
the Welsh Office in Cardiff. Her four collections of poetry are
Crowded by Shadows (1977), *What a Place to Grow Flowers* (1980),
Earth Studies and Other Voyages (1983) and *Beware Falling Tor-
toises* (1987); her *Selected Poems* appeared in 1990. She has also
published a volume of verse translated from the French and
German, *Prisoners of Transience* (1985), and won the Babel Prize
for Translation in 1984.

OLIVER REYNOLDS   Born in Cardiff in 1957. He studied
Drama at Hull University and then worked in the theatre. He
has published two collections of verse: *Skevington's Daughter*
(1985) and *The Player Queen's Wife* (1987); the latter included
the long poem, 'Rorschach Writing', with which he won the
Arvon Foundation International Poetry Competition in 1985.

GRAHAM THOMAS   Born in Abertyleri, Monmouthshire, in 1944, educated at the University College of Wales, Aberystwyth. He is Head of the Faculty of Science and Mathematics in the comprehensive school of his home-town. His first collection of poetry is *The One Place* (1983).

CHRIS TORRANCE   Born in Edinburgh in 1941, settled in Glyn Neath in 1970. He lives as a writer and part-time tutor. The poems he has selected are from *The Magic Door*, of which four parts have so far appeared – *The Magic Door* (1975), *Citrinas* (1977), *The Diary of Palug's Cat* (1980) and *The Book of Brychan* (1982).

JOHN POWELL WARD   Born in Suffolk in 1937, educated at the Universities of Toronto, Cambridge and Wales. He was a lecturer ·in Education at University College, Swansea, from 1963 to 1989, but has now retired and lives in Kent. His five collections of poetry are *The Other Man* (1968), *The Line of Knowledge* (1972), *From Alphabet to Logos* (1972), *To Get Clear* (1981) and *The Clearing* (1984). He has also published an essay on Raymond Williams in the *Writers of Wales* series and two critical studies, *Poetry and the Sociological Idea* (1981) and *Wordsworth's Language of Men* (1984). From 1975 to 1980 he was editor of the magazine *Poetry Wales*.

NIGEL WELLS   Born in Northampton in 1944, educated at the University College of Wales, Aberystywyth; he lives in Machynlleth, Powys. He has published three collections of verse: *Venturing Out from Trees* (1970), *The Winter Festivals* (1980) and *Wilderness/Just Bounce* (1988); with the last he won a Welsh Arts Council Prize in 1989.

PENNY WINDSOR   Born in 1946 and brought up in the West Country; she has been living in Swansea for more than twenty years. She has worked as a teacher and youth worker, and for the National Association of Citizens' Advice Bureaux, but now lives as a writer. Her two collections of verse are *Dangerous Women* (1987) and *Like Oranges* (1989).

The Bright Field

I have seen the sun break through
to illuminate a small field
for a while, and gone my way
and forgotten it. But that was the pearl
of great price, the one field that had
the treasure in it. I realize now
that I must give all that I have
to possess it. Life is not hurrying

on to a receding future, nor hankering after
an imagined past. It is the turning
aside like Moses to the miracle
of the lit bush, to a brightness
that seemed as transitory as your youth
once, but is the eternity that awaits you.

R.S. THOMAS

BRYAN ASPDEN

For me Wales is movement. Like the painter John Petts in 'Fallen Pines' I got here thinking I'd arrived, and then discovered that learning and knowing a place is another journey: only when you've settled as though to a centre, however shifting, can you stretch out past national edges to international sympathy, as he did to Alabama, to Sharpeville. Some people stay all their life without arriving. The voter I canvassed in 'A Rum Game', with the carefully tended elsewhere of his garden, a kind of Home Counties-cum-Llys Crystenin, was growing ever more detached as he watched what he believed was real, his own corner of a lasting empire, drift away from him. I've been to many exhibitions of 'Water Colours' where people have painted a Wales which is – where they came from before things started to go wrong, where they'll go again if they're good: but the real anywhere, where we have to live and grow, starts outside these dreamlands. Learning Welsh, I learned the shift between, not two selves perhaps, but different issues of the self, one in hard, the other in soft covers, that is recorded in 'Which We Are'. The necessary misunderstandings that enable a country to get on with itself are by now so close to second nature, we need the drop-out Kyffin Williams was for a period in 'Pentrepella' to show them to us. Reading his autobiography, I followed his escape from both sides of our contention, the way he had to go before he could discover, or invent, where he came from.

And being here, not bothered by it, is where I start the same journey. The echoes hurtle back, by InterCity train. Durham Castle and Cathedral passed the carriage window as I opened the thirties, 'Vin Audenaire' fizzing over John Lehmann's *London Magazine*. They were mature then. Old, they have life to combat the resurgent meanness and greyness we thought they'd done for. On the way from southern Spain to Scunthorpe, between trains in Paris, I walked all night through the streets around St Lazare. I recognized the fog-lit life I saw there when decades later I glanced through a book of Picasso's early gouaches, one of them 'Blind Man's Meal'. In Spain itself I caught fading echoes of the Civil War, 'eat your bread or you'll die', which grow stronger with subsequent histories. 'October Again' and 'Leaving the Party Early' can only stand witness here for what we still have to learn.

A Rum Game

Anchorage, High Winds, the place
where wrought iron dolphins swam
above Harbour View – I crossed them
off my register and went
from the last house in Gannock Park
to the first in Gannock Park West.
In through the double gates, ignoring
the bark and the twitched chain, and trying

to make no noise on the crunchy gravel.
He was standing behind the Mexican
Orange Blossom, with a bedding plant
and a trowel, hoping to finish a border
while the weather kept fine. 'Plaid?'
He shook hands limply with the leaflet I offered.

Tapering, he might have stood
for the flagpole I'd expected on his lawn
though the breath of a Whisky Mac
was all that fluttered in the slight breeze.
'Some good points – the language – half
a Welshman myself,' he huffed, and hawed
a word about the election. Then the garden
he'd bought as a young man thirty years ago
and was lost in now. Neither of us mentioned
the double first in history and drink
who'd have his vote. 'Nice meeting you.
Go that way if you like. It's a rum game.'
I went down a path of cinders, leafmould,
past the groundsel, out through a leaning gate.

Pentrepella – Kyffin Williams

'Nid yw'r graig yn siarad Saesneg'
('The rocks don't understand English') – Bethesda saying

Like mud from the beudy
it was not to be brought indoors,
the language farmers used
to talk about bulls and the birth of calves.
Even your father,
who only came alive in Welsh,
had to scrape it off at the doorstep.

Taidi's house – one patched eye,
the other stuck to his telescope –
was kind to the old words that dawdled
among thrift, sea campion,
crempog teas on the farms, and the Liverpool liners
washing the Skerries.

But grandfather's – who relished his diary:
'No sermon today, owing to my throat.
The year ends with gloomy prospect,
owing to Transvaal war' –
could not stomach their half-dressed carollings and chirpings.

School in Trearddur, where the wind slipped its tracts
under the doors of holiday cottages.
Days on the hills with Bonzo,
or loafing on Moel y Gest in the sun.
Then the lost years of elocution
at Shrewsbury, four-mile runs
and beatings over hot water pipes.
After a botched tonsillectomy
you gave up trying
and drifted as far from words
as your eyes could carry.

Your brother started his career.
They found you articles with Yale and Hardcastle
off the High Street, Pwllheli.
Land agents of the old school –
mornings tootling round the estates,
then a meet with the Border Counties
or a rough shoot at Nanhoron.
One night in the Anglesea Arms –
You'd been out after duck on the Afon Wen –
a glass of port, Sospan Fach, the Old Grey Mare –
you woke under the snow
on your bedroom floor,
blood in your mouth, your tongue
a bolster stuffed with pain.

The doctor prescribed
Belladonna, luminal, Irish Moss;
gave instructions not to use your brain
to excess. You joined the Royal Welch Fusiliers
as a Second Lieutenant.
The War took you from Pwllheli to Porthmadog,
across the water to Lurgan
and back, your troops labelled
'Passenger to Pwllheli. I speak no English.'
Six months at Maentwrog

pretending what to do
if the Germans came.
But no dodging the Grand Mal.
'You can't play sir, you're not well,'
as they carried you foaming
from the rugby field.
The medical board found you abnormal
and discharged you to the Slade.

A half world of the Home Guard
and figure drawing.
Three days teaching a week.
You found it comfy, having no talent
and no one to push you.
On dull evenings
drawn by the light behind a roof ridge,
the sheen of wet slate,
you painted your way to Wales.
Even Miss Jopling's half-blind cooking –
bread, butter and marmalade cat hairs,
your morning kipper grilled
in the News of the World –
could not stop you following hounds
down tongues of water
after make-believe otters.

You watched the cliffs break against the sea
at Capel Tywyn,
slept where the Ynysfor taps
gushed midnight Guinness.
At Bisham Gardens, N6, you learned
to talk to the rocks
in their own language.

Water Colours

In the old reading room, where the unemployed
angled like herons over the job columns
for a trout from that sluggish stream,
and afternoon drunks snoozed
over *Y Faner* and *The Church Times*,
there's an exhibition this week: Water Colours
by Local Artists. Each frame's enclosed
a babble of green fields in rural Wales
where all roads are lanes, hedges layered or grown
to a cave of leaves. There's no barbed wire;
no bedstead mending a gap in the stone wall.
No traffic; no tourists. Almost, it seems,
no people – except that the farms are cared for
and the cottages have just been whitewashed.

Walking deeper in water colour land
I mark these occupations: a tractor,
driven by two brush strokes of tweed
and the smudge of a cap, ploughing a field.
A farmer herding sheep with two dogs, no landrover.
In late summer a post van parks by the farmyard.
Its scarlet complements the overflow
of green. Then heat-hazy hills; the first cornet notes
of September birch trees, tuning up
for the tone poem, 'Autumn Tints'.
And now in this room it's winter. White swathes
cumber the fields and we are cold,
in a land without a language, whose troubles lie
outside the frame with its red circle 'sold'.

Which We Are

Gwynt-y-Mynydd creaks like its own footsteps
on the stairs. Rain taps the roof.
We live inside a drum and we are part
of the music that we're listening to.
Under the clouded pewter of the winter skies
the mountain comes closer, pushing

humped fields with their boulder scree of sheep.
When it's almost dark Trefor has a choice
of Mad Dan Dado with his matchstick spaceship
or Un Llygoden Fach waving his cutlass
over a translated Armada. Five more minutes
one for each year, then it's 'amser'. He concentrates
on wasting nothing. 'Tell me a story', he asks.
'Tell it in Welsh or English, which we are.'

Fallen Pines

for John Petts

Your journey started
when you got off the train
and came to a halt on the platform,
wondering which way was forward.

A slow walk uphill
as Aber pelted down,
till you reached a house
shelved on the Carneddau.

in Hafod-y-Gelyn you learned
to cut valleys in wood
and sharpen ridges to print
tracks a farmer leaves

on soil two horses have opened.
They know what they're doing,
these fat rumps and heavy heads
bent to their footwork, this hand

throwing seed higher than Moel Wnion.
While the face turned by April sun,
gormless with resurrection,
doesn't check where it falls.

Pine roots in air fill a winter picture;
and one man – thumbsized, but all lines point
where he's crouched in snow
sawing logs for a fire.

Other trades fuelled your painting:
pithead gear, with helmets lowered
to crop an older wood
and wearing light to work by,

caged light whose colours cry
between steel bars 'You do it to ME' –
words your stained Christ would shout
from an Alabama window.

Sharpeville or plastic bullets
nail him to his tree. His body bends
on the crossbeam of a water cannon
that lifts his arms in air.

Did it have to be such pain
turned his face to the light?
Is there no other way
hands can touch Heaven?

Vin Audenaire

It would be nice to sit and drink again
in some Berliner Bahnhof Bistro
Vin Audenaire and Wisherwater.

New Year's Eve at Olga's. Tomorrow, Paris –
Mr Norris changes toupées at the border.
'Drop in for Himbeergeist or a Prairie Oyster.'

Yes, I remember the thirsties:
Streetfights, brownshirts, Blue Riders and the Threepenny Opera
while the Reichsmark dips and sinks.

Bogeyed from dosshouse, soup kitchen,
with a false passport and a new name,
blond herrenvolkporn in his pocket

on a park bench where lindens drip,
an arts dropout dole addict
does up his duffle and dreams of Sturm und Drang.

'Back Britain, bugger blacks,
restore Biggles, birch, roast beef
and Rupert Brooke.'

Twilight of the Gods? Valhalla?
Open the cabinet. Pour a doctored stiffener.
Wolf it down and Tebbit on.

Blind Man's Meal

(i)
Paintings to light the gas with
or warm the stove on nights
when Clichy's gloved with fog
and fingers do time to colonize
fresh wastes of paper.

(ii)
Lazarus Station, last train gone.
Railway police with batons
tickle the ribs of midnight dossers
and raise them from their benches
in dead cold. Gagged with sleep they argue
wrongs without words and rights mislaid
then pick themselves up and go
downhill, through streets where rags
find their level, caught on a grid
in the Metro's caporale.

Cheapest colour's the pale blue
mother's face
who walks with her baby
to Mary's house to strain for mercy:
'Lady be good
between la Trinité and Madeleine'
but goodness is in the dark, behind the back
of Sister Sanctimony whose smile
holds the door above worn steps.

They stumble, and scrape forward,
arms and hands a thin hedge,
November fruit
hugging its thorn.

(iii)
Seventy-three strikes, and winter has taken
what the army left
from the shelves.
In the café's dusk
all you can see by is a face
lighting a table.
Water, soup, a stale roll –
your eyes were hungry for the blind man's meal.
They scrape the bowl,
break the crust and fall
on skin pinched
over wrist, knuckles, fingers that reach
the jug's handle,
tasting its roughness and glaze.

(iv)
Grotsville under construction
but no shelter yet.
On a traceroad's open stage
street actors accept their dusty welcome
and settle on rubble chairs
to unpack their props:
hoop, wings, a ball to balance on –
borders that have crossed them
and states they can't get into
have taught them
to take their living lightly.

Drum tap, barker's cry,
an audience conjures itself up
and the ball starts rolling.

Harlequin insect thin;
clown's double-bellied suit;
a body whose bulges
are the last resort of muscle
before plasticine –
trumped up wrestler wrapped in chains
he shouts and sweats for freedom
till the chains fall
with a drizzle of small change and grubby notes
to pick up and start again.

Rose madder nudging blue

(v)
Paintings to line the bank with
and stretch an afternoon
of tepid waves at Cannes
when all that fingers can frame
is not cheating.

October Again

From 'Blackening to Goya', a sequence on the Spanish Civil War

October again, and war
survives the cold and falling leaves.
Artillery traces red pools.
Trees are empty as streets.
You watch all night till the sun
flowers in their branches.
A wood is blasted from the earth.
You are a tree still standing.
Autumn, and now winter.
The tree hasn't a stitch to its name
and the sun has stopped calling.
You stay there, dry, cold, yellow,
green under ground.

Leaving the Party Early

From 'Blackening to Goya', a sequence on the Spanish Civil War

Leaving the party early you took
someone else's coat from the stand
and then the wrong road home.

'Off already?' But hurrying on,
you didn't hear me. My voice caught
in the sound of the river, carried
by a wind so ahead of itself
it might have been your fate
shrugged from your shoulders and looking
where to settle.

When I found you by the roadside
a small red flower
crazing your forehead, your eyes
in terror of fire,
it was as if my own death had died
handing me this life
I was at a loss what to do with
so many years to add to mine
and fill with struggle
knowing what I'd have to earn
before paying them back to earth.

JOHN BARNIE

I was brought up in Abergavenny, Gwent, in the 1940s and '50s. My family belonged to what is now an almost vanished sub-class, the small-town shopkeeper. Their world gave me a strong sense of certainty, and a confidence in a very restricted identity, both of which were to be eroded by later experience.

However, the town is surrounded by hills – Skirrid Fawr, Skirrid Fach, the Blorenge, Llanwenarth Breast, the Rholben, the Deri. I couldn't walk in the town and not be aware of their presence. In winter, under snow, they shone like full, white sails; they were black and sharp on summer nights. The hills had a high ceremonial of their own which had a daily influence on my life at the time.

I began to write after I had lived in cities for several years, partly because nothing I experienced there gave me the intensity I associated with my Abergavenny past; but also because the two aspects of that intensity – the life of the small town, and the bare, dominant mass of the hills – left me feeling divided against myself and dissatisfied.

Many of the poems I've written are about nature and about the difference between us as humans and nature. The Romantic poets interest me because of this, especially Coleridge with his strong sense of the rift between the completeness of nature and the unfulfilled self.

In 1985 I moved to Comins Coch, near Aberystwyth, a village that looks out on Pumlumon and Bryn Garw, hills that are bleaker than the ones I grew up with. They are the setting for poems like 'At Craig-y-Pistyll'.

But the focus of my writing has gradually shifted. It is hard to experience pleasure in nature when it is being destroyed all around me. I want to know more now about the mind that can do this. Ironically, it has led me back to the small town, where people connived gladly all my life at nature's destruction, calling it progress.

Once I thought I could escape the past, but the past, it seems, always keeps faith. It is there now, like the shadow under my heels, in whatever I write.

Encounter

Swallows flitting low
Over the grass, swimming
At our waists like
Blue-black-electric fish

Silent and buoyant, lighter
Than the air they
Breathe, gliding
Among the boles of trees.

We stand, rooted,
Or make as if to wade
Through the evening,
Heavy in our lives,

While the swallows flick
On razor wings then
Dive, air's dolphins,
Shadowing the ground.

Etruscan

Interfectus est: the perfect ending.
Power like an irritation in the bone
Drove the general on, a speartip stilled him.

Now he goes begging the other side
Of forgetting, in a toga, with a bowl
Empty of its offerings of meat, bread and wine.

Jowled, the neckskin slack, in lizard-
Folds from living well, he's more banker
Than lord. Hard for him to live in Hell.

To lie supine, while in effigy, in tufa,
He reclines on an elbow, bowl held off-
Handedly, arrogantly, on a paunchful of stone.

Patient Griselda

There's a wealth in seabirds
Pouring behind the plough,
And white sheets spread out to dry
On bushes of privet.

Radiance is from the heart,
The eye's beams turning back
To the beholder, so what she sees
She is. Scrubbing flagstones

Is a means to purity,
The foot-worn stones effaced,
Hard and yielding. My husband
Has a savage eye, asks questions,

Lives in shadows. To him
The owl's hoot is the mind's cry;
The children kicking leaves
Are suspect. He must

Knead and knead the living dough,
But cannot eat the bread. He says
I should live like him in shadow,
And hates me for the light.

Home Town

I think of the widows; closed flowers.
Who will find them lovely, remembering
Life in the withered petals of their lips.
In morning coffee rooms
They crowd like memories, sunnily.
The make-up and the perms suggest
Summer frocks and jaunts before the war.
Now they tread to church and pray
For company. They are delicate, like moths
Found clinging to the panes on autumn
Nights. Their powdered cheeks are soft
As downy wings. Their eyes glitter
Like gems in faded boxes, blue, green,
And on fire, as many years ago.

How to Watch Birds

Shallows of the sea frozen over in sheets,
Crackling panes of ice that split, squeaked under foot,
And in between, wrinkled sand like buried ribs.
The tide was turning, sneaking in under the ice,
Cold runs of water like the clearest crystal.
We walked on the sand, wavered, slid, on the creaking sea,
And a steely wind tortured tears from our eyes,
So the world wobbled, flashed ripple-light
Off water and ice, while the cold dug deep
Into our bones, and the wind hammered our skulls.
Doug had brought brandy which we drained in large gulps,
And the glow-coloured liquid left us no warmer.
We were defeated. But the great black-backed gulls,
Redshanks and shelducks and barrel-chested geese
Stayed on, foursquare on ice or seafrozen stones,
Staring into the wind. We lurched, lunged back
                    to the road.
          My head banged with pain
          The cap of bone too cold
          To touch, the wrinkled brain
          Hunched in its hole, like a toad.

November Storm

Wind heading east today
With a job to do; trees
To uproot, and slates to flip
Like crazy coins from the roofs.

There's a roaring in the air
Miles deep, and the birds are gone,
Except the ground-level sparrows
Slap-dashed into shelter.

This is the time I like,
The light sharp steel in a moil
Of clouds, any second to snap
And spin into the ground. The city

Hunkers in mud,
Crude as a kraal,
And all our expensive lives
Lie down with fear.

The Death of King Arthur

When Arthur speared his nephew bastard son
Two feet through the guts, and Mordred *threste hymselff*
With alle the myght he had, up to the guard
On the old King's lance, then struck him to the brain,

A redshank probed the margins of the lake, dipping
Its head and breast, as if they hinged on its long red legs,
Sounding for molluscs in the stagnant mud. And when
The sun went down, and *robbers and pyllours* worked among the
     dead,

The sky was shot with stars, blazing and trailing
Through deepening space. So the large-eyed night creatures
Sniffed round the harness, the useless fingers and eyes,
Scuttling at dawn down holes, into the dark, red earth.

Blake's Dreams

1
I'll burn through these doors. The universe is – is –
The mind's a mantrap – most tread gingerly
Afraid it will spring. I'd hang gladly
To leap into the world within.
Life was never a prison to me.
Sapience – restraint, control – chains melt
In the mind's acetylene flare.
You, you, and you, who know nothing.
Sparks shower from the cutting edge,
Dance and bounce on the floor. – Soon to be through! –

You'll not look – but I'll look –
I'll splinter your parallelograms –
Words in your book will darken and burn –
I'll stand and be elected by the light.

2
Look at this now... acid's snaky lines;
It's the devil's work dissolving metal.
Such dilutions... careful calculations.
And all for an imprint on the page
Of my dreams. – Half of you to spurn them,
Fall into death and rot –
The natural way with mankind.
You'll have plenty of prophets –
Bible-Jacks who drink cold water
And vomit lies. Who stands for truth
Must pass the test himself – plunge in
Head and shoulders through the flames.
You see nothing... but I see a treadmill
Rattling in sunlight to a flurry of feet.

Mary Shelley

Like a sycamore's winged seed, brought down –
'Are you that damned atheist Shelley?'
Three children buried should have been enough.
Post-haste – the wheels of his carriage
Clatter across Italy. In the *maremma* the frogs –
Grex-grex, grex-grex. He told the men of England
In no uncertain terms.... In his glass tower
He could see the wind build storms.
Peace, miserable peace; his name was a byword;
Whenever was there peace for me.
Show me your scars, mine stretch across my belly.
The doors are open for a wind to blow in,
Cooling my face and ruffling the curtains.
We never closed them anywhere we lived....
Books, bundled into coaches, boxes,
Left scattered, called for, lost; like letters
Never arriving and perhaps not sent.

Father was a better dun than the courts,
Shelley's banknotes, gold and drafts kept him,
A door onto a ruin, implacable.
Someone lived there once. My mother?
Byron eats biscuits to keep the body thin,
But the souls of these poets are fat, fat.
Shelley comes and asks, 'Shall we dress for dinner?
I'm tired of this *déshabillé.'*
The noble lords of England! Throw down the whip,
There's still the spur. And the frogs go
Grex, grex-grex, grex-grex, grex...grex.

Clay

(Coleridge)

'Promise.' I was a fine sight, setting out.
I could annotate a book in minutes,
Fillet the thought from the words' integument.
It was a party trick – friends clapped,
Lent me their books to be marginally glossed.
I could quote 'auctoritee' till midnight.
Last night the moon lay hidden by a cloud,
A dark, uncomprehending mass; but light
Brightened its edges, streamed into the sky
Softening the gloom. I waited minutes,
Minutes.... The cloud was a sullen beast,
The one I have felt upon my back
Deadening my joy, turning me to clay.
I stood then as if looking at myself.

We're all wandering, though some don't know it.
William looks at me down his long thin nose:
'Not I my friend.' We haven't met in years....
I remember his disapproving glance.
Why am I the failure? His verse goes on
Like well-intentioned knitting. My life
Revolved round plans, I was the architect,
Blueprints of the mind scattered about.
Friends looked in to admire the proposition:

'This will be great.' Everything was mind,
Platonic, a vast uncharted land.
I grappled with immense ideas. Applause!
Prometheus must come to earth with fire.
Who set store by an empty-handed hero?

Leaving

The new life!
It seems like every turn
Opens a vista: those hills!
That estuary! People –

At the end of the journey
Suitcase unpacked,
There's the same old face
To be shaved,

Barefaced, there's the same
Old lie. It's hard
To change. The good thief
Was too good; the bad

Like most, hoped
Against the chance
That at sundown events
Would set him free.

'I never knew.'
'I never thought.'
The leopard washed in soap's
As good as new,

As old. He looks around.
Cut from the cross,
Wounds healed, the thief
Turns corners, steals again.

Grass

Even a lawn
As it whimpers underfoot
Inches sideways –

Not like a sycophant
But one with a grasp on things. Cut back,
Chopped out,

Grass plays small
In the shadow of man.

Left a year, lawns riot to
Tussocks,
Uncombable shambles.

We prefer clipped dress,
But a lawn's *déshabillé*
Is right

For the rough lout, steaming in November sun,
Dumb and sullen
Under frost.

Grass waits.
Even the keenest mower dies,
And over his grave

Humped like a mummy-case
Or flat like a door
It will grow

The mower's last green coat.

Parallel Lines

What a surprise:
The white surface
Of the moon, a face
In shock, hair torn off,

On what I thought
Was an ordinary
Day, floating in blue.
And here come gulls

In a keen cruise,
Intent on their doings
Like the motion
Of silence.

Blood and bone
Keep me trudging
While the gulls spill air
To harbour in a field

And the moon
Fades as if the future
Were a self-effacement
Into the past.

At Craig-y-Pistyll

At Craig-y-Pistyll there's a deserted house
This side of the rocky gully that takes excess water from the dam.
With the door ajar and burst from its hinges
I didn't need to knock before I went in,
And black-and-red tiles in square patterns
Led me to the living-room where grey light from a small window
Showed me tools with smooth handles no one had a use for,
And a long-shafted spade for pulling bread deftly from the oven
In a deep recess by the grate. And there were chairs, unvarnished,
And looking as though they were made to be patient in.

In the kitchen nothing but bare stone, and bottles on a shelf,
Green and brown glass with dust round the necks.
Going up the dried wood of the narrow stairs
Was still like intruding on a privacy,
Bending to peer through dirty panes in low windows,
Wandering the four rooms across echoing planks.
But there were holes in the roof where slates had slipped
And the open sky was a greater intrusion.
In the shed outside there had been sheets of hardboard,
Beams of rough-cut wood (none of it new),
The hardboard buckling slightly from being stacked
At too broad an angle against the wall.
And wandering into a final bedroom
I found a double-bed wrapped in black polythene.
Lying back, I stared through a hole in the roof
And listened to wind in nearby trees.
Whoever had been here with the timber and hardboard
Had lain as well on the damp-free shining mattress and slept,
Or not slept but turned at last on his back to look at the clouds
    flushed by the moon
And clusters of stars that could have been galaxies
Shimmering faintly in the holes above his head.
Then he heard the silence as defined by leaves
And the intricate movements of a stream meandering in shallows
    a hundred yards from the house.
The bread spade, the useless tools and the stripped farmhouse
    chairs had been his,
Not the left-overs of people giving up and leaving the door open
    without looking back
Following the bitter jutting of their jaws.
Even in summer he felt chilly on the bed
And at dawn got up for breakfast, too much like camping,
Then went to the shed and set-to at his work.
Whenever he stopped, the hush of the trees entered him.
He listened, started again, leaned to the wood as the saw bit
    through his pencil line.
A man can be absorbed by a place until he lives its life, wears
    its face,
Looks out the door warily with its eyes.
That last night he lay on the black bed and knew this,
Got up next day and walked down the track past the one workable
    farm,
Over the stepping stones of the stream,

Up the path that cuts across a spur of the hill,
Then along the grass lane until he came to Salem, where
As the tarmac passed hurriedly under the shadow of his feet
He took himself again to be the person that he was.

DUNCAN BUSH

I made my final choices for this book largely on thematic grounds. I've chosen poems which seem to me to reflect consistent concerns and which inhabit what is by and large an identifiably contemporary world. If some of these are 'political' poems – and several could be thought to be – what they might have in common here (or at any rate what lies behind them) is probably less a sense of particular shades of political administration than a recognition of a universe increasingly *administered*, and in increasingly successful ways. A universe where specifics count (as they still do, and have to), but where physical distances, like whole topographies of cultural difference, have shrunk. Television waves travel faster than poems (than even intercontinental missiles).

In a number of these poems my choice also reflects an experience which is essentially urban (or suburban). I've written poems on more rural themes. But the urban, industrial and maritime (or inter-cultural) experience of the capital has, after all, been paramount – demographically, politically, socially – in any history of modern Wales. This is also true in the case of my own biography, as a native of that almost cynically realistic, cosmopolitan city of Cardiff.

It goes without saying that such poetry seeks to fly by those ranged nets of nostalgia and local colourism, not to mention other forms of Celtic Moonshine.

In the end, poetry feeds on the real. You have to dig where you stand.

But you must also dig where the imagination bids you travel; my book, *The Genre of Silence*, is set in the Soviet Union during the Stalin years; a recent sequence deals with a traumatized veteran of the American war in Vietnam. Neither of these forays into the still-unexpunged nightmares of modern history has anything whatsoever to do with Wales (rural, urban, or otherwise). And why should they?

The truth is that poets anywhere do most of their digging seated at a writing-desk.

Nevertheless – given the space available, and in the context of what *is* to be an anthology of Welsh poetry – I've omitted these particular longer works from consideration here (with the single exception of the poem 'The Galley'). I mention other work since a brief selection is inevitably almost more aware of what it has to leave out than of what it includes.

Beyond that, simply to choose poems that might declare their place and meaning out of a doubtful decade has seemed as good a guiding principle as any other.

Poem for Joe

Six months after the birth each
night hourly we go up
still to overhear
your breathing: stooping
into the dim cot, intent as
for the heartbeat.

Little egg, soft nape, unstirring
eyelashes, the pale fuzz
you were born with
shadows your head's
dome, profiled
perfect as a lightbulb's,

while your life
swings on that one, fine
hair
of imperceptible breath...
Until a tiny, sprawled hand
twitches, or (disturbed

between what dreams?) you lug
your head facing
the other way: four-legged
in your primrose
terry Baby-Gro,
still clumsy as a tortoise.

Gently I creak out backwards
on the floorboards.
For new parents each
child sleeps the sleep
of innocence and of
the just – the only just.

Crocuses

In the seconds after
the knock he may have
tried to burn the poem
that would kill him. But
words are hard to kill. Print turned
silvery as the page went black.

They put him in the big
house on the outskirts with
white bedsteads and no
windows. But word
went down the heating pipes,
leaked out through
even screamproofed walls.

In the end someone probably
shot him on a train
going east, or just off it,
and hid the body in the
ground. Here and there his
words came slowly up like
crocuses, in winter.

Pneumoconiosis

This is the dust:

black diamond dust.

I had thirty years in it, boy,
a laughing red mouth
coming up to spit smuts black
into a handkerchief.

But it's had forty years
in me now:
so fine
you could inhale it

through a gag.
I'll die with it now.
It's in me,
like my blued scars.

But I try not think about it.

I take things pretty easy, these days;
one step at a time.
Especially the stairs.
I try not to think about it.

I saw my own brother: rising,
dying in panic, gasping
worse than a hooked carp
drowning in air.
Every breath was his last
till the last.

I try not to think about it. But

know me by my slow step,
the occasional little cough, involuntary
and delicate as a consumptive's,

and my lung full of budgerigars.

Coming Back

Every time you come back
it has shrunk again, as if
the railings had closed in
on the park, or

the roads had shortened
their perspectives;
as if the hills had come
nearer like clouds.

It's not only what had not
been there, nor what's
missing: once all of this
seemed vast, was known.

Suddenly farness of things,
the space they occupy, is
altered here,
is unimaginably less

than memory. And everything
is bigger than this suburb
you were born in, even
the one you have to live in now.

Café, Rainy Tuesday Morning

The boy keeps his cup of
dregs on the formica tabletop

in front of him as if
it were a ticket for admission.

He nurses it close to
his hands when the old man

comes clearing tables.
It's a white, semi-translucent

cup, the kind you always get
in cafés. People

go and come. But others
stay, like him. He's

not the only one. Today
he's got the table by the street.

He taps a wrinkled
cigarette made from the tin's dust.

The urn steams. The plateglass
steams. Again

he clears a segment
of it with his sleeve,

a windscreen-wiper's shape.
He's heading nowhere

fast, his father keeps on
telling him. He only knows it's slow,

too slow. It's not yet even
noon, and there's no future

in his tealeaves.
He bought *The Sun* this morning,

but it's rolled up
on the table near his cup. Now

and then absently he'll pick
it up and furl

it tighter in his two hands,
almost like you'd wring

a chicken's neck. The newsprint's
soiled

his fingers, but that's all
it's good for now. He

doesn't get it for the jobs. One
thing he's learning, that

it's hard to make a daily paper
last all day.

Bardot in Grangetown

Off Ferry Road, the toilet of a garage where
the mechanics come at lunch to cut the hands' grease
with green Swarfega jelly, glancing once

at themselves in the rust-foxed mirror, and then
go in to eat brought sandwiches and play
pontoon with the soft, soiled pack,

three walls of the cubicle sporting the odd grey
newsprint pinup, some 'Kay' or 'Tracy'
(alike as playing cards)

and then a whole closed door facing you if
ever you sat over the stained bowl
of Bardot as she was at twenty,

and thirty-five, and is now, in her smiling
puppy-fat fifties, still corn-blonde
and then more of her

again (with one of Ian Rush) out where they eat,
over the workbench's oil and
hacksaw-dust, the clenched vice.

The boy who put all hers up was a six-month
Government trainee. A bit simple, they all thought.
A headbanger, the fat one said.

He had a thing about her, the boy, grinning
foolishly, half-proudly, if they kidded him, told him
she was old enough to be

his mother. *That slag?* the fat one said once.
*Look at her. She's anybody's. Even saving baby seals
all she knows how to do*

is lie down with one. And laughed: soft, smirched face
looking at that photo, then at the one of
her naked, hands raised as if to pin or

loose her hair, the honey-hued, still-teenage
body, milky Mediterranean behind her, evening.
He left the other week,

the trainee. He didn't finish, never even came
back for his tools. So now they're
anybody's, like the photos:

like, the fat one knows, the photos always are.

Pull-in

They know her, easy,
from the drab ill-fitting shoes,
that sullen tough look or
one pale bare leg's faint
blue nubeculae of bruise,

like thumbprints fading
out through hues of iodine.
She re-crosses those flagrant legs,
shifts gum across her mouth,
re-chews it. Sixteen? Seventeen?

The shoe-heel swings free
from her lifted, wrinkled sole,
a picked scab where the upper
must have worn her last
tights to a hole

just beneath the tendon.
Absently her toes flex
to the jukebox's dull bass-line.
She waits on, hardly in time. What
she's rife with's not so much sex

as an aleatory boredom
up and down the motorways,
in gravel lorry-parks and Little Chefs.
The arm whirs, re-selects and
drops: Hendrix, and 'Purple Haze'.

Her youth's composed of
these anachronistic hits
made hers by proxy. She outstares
and then ignores you, as
her driver comes back, sits,

gets up to slot a coin
in the machine against the wall.
He sways, slams, joggles. She's sprung
flippers, bumpers, arches,
pivots. He's the shiny silver ball.

Hot Estate Sunday

The man sits smoking on the step
in shorts, next to the righted racing-bike
stripped, oiled and cleaned.
A television set
surges amid gunfire
in the empty room, its blowy windows open.
To his own eye, looking down,
he's already browner
than he is, and the terracotta
chimney-pots now burn
with evening.
His kid plays on
the hairy scrap of lawn. It's half
in shadow.
When he finishes
this cigarette, he'll wheel the bike
inside and wash,
put on a clean coloured shirt
and take the slow
walk to the new, brick pub.

Sometimes he arrives
foot-perfect, as the bolts go back
at 7.
He'll drink tonight until the sky is black.

The Sunday the Power Went Off

In a darkening house we sat,
room-light gone, television shrunk
mid-shout to a speck then

nothing, even the old fridge's
whir and periodic
judder stilled,

and saw each other in
flashlight instants while
my five-year-old elder son

counted the sulphur-violet
dimness and I with him:
One. Two. Three. Four. Five:

a second for each year
of his life, and the sum for every
mile as slowly the storm

moved off to a horizon
of rumbles from that sudden
crack in the sky that seemed

right over the roof-ridge
like the rifleshot amplifying
down a badlands canyon

in movies, the one-off, perfect shot
bringing a man unexpectedly down
forever, though the sunlight

unimpaired, the reel
unfinished, the shocked wildlife
listening a second more then

resuming its tiny business
of survival, even the dead man's
skewbald reaching down to

browse the seeding grass.
Storms now scare me more than
my half-scared, half-excited kids,

if only that first, premonitory
skyquake, distant and dull
as a range of hills or

that dark low cloud like hills
you get at dusk; that, or
the faint first flash I know

may any time come before a roar
as of wind and of whirlwind,
finding me sitting

in this same stone house or bending
in the sunlit garden, knowing
instantly under clear air

this wasn't lightning, seeing
wife, sons, sunlight suddenly
reversed, as in a negative,

and simply waiting with them there,
too scared this time to count.

The Galley

Let some have whips and wear uniform.
Let some have oars and wear rag. Let these
be more. So have them shackled
at ankle and wrist. Let the galley

move. The immense effort of shifting
inert mass through the sea is well known.
A strange thing is, those
in the uniform think it's the strokes

of the whip which achieve it.

GILLIAN CLARKE

It's not easy to be your own editor. The task set me rummaging in the rag-and-bone-shop of the heart, rereading the bare inch my own pages take up between Clare and Clemo on my shelves. It doesn't look much. Few of the poems completely satisfy me now. Some surprise me. Some uncover images that still gleam. None tells lies. Each poem is a journal entry to record the way I thought, what I saw, with dark pages between where nine poems out of ten were discarded along the way.

I pass over the apprentice pieces from the first full collection. My favourites have already been too much anthologized, the rest were artlessly, instinctively written, and that mood ended with publication. Instead I begin at the end of 'Letter from a Far Country', one of my first deliberate poems. It was written intensely in five late-night sessions, to the muffled drum-beats of my teenage children. It's a protest for and celebration of the women in my family and the places where they lived, and a lament for their lost ways of living, fiction made of truth and fact laid over each other like photographs taken without winding on the film. It was the last of my indoorscapes. The children left home, the far countries came closer. I became a traveller and could choose my subjects from a wider world. 'Cofiant' is a journey into my forefathers' lives, the men's story. The original Cofiant was written about my great-great grandfather, Thomas Williams, Baptist Minister, father of nineteen children, born in Llŷn in 1800. The book gave me my ancestors and saved their lives for me. From the sequence of poems I select 'Thomas Williams', and 'John Penri Williams', my father, wireless engineer, about whom I have begun to write at last, thirty years after his early death. 'The Hare' celebrates friendship, companionable, generous and long-lasting, and is an elegy for the death of Frances Horovitz. Its sense of our animal mortality still shocks me when I read it aloud. 'Llŷr' records one of the experiences that made me a writer, one of those falling-in-love with words moments that charge language with private meaning and fuse the experience of the ten-year-old child with that of the middle-aged woman. 'Neighbours' warns; 'Seal' praises; 'Overheard in County Sligo' makes a feminist nursery-rhyme out of a scrap of eavesdropping.

The Hare

i.m. Frances Horovitz 1938-1983

That March night I remember how we heard
a baby crying in a neighbouring room
but found him sleeping quietly in his cot.

The others went to bed and we sat late
talking of children and the men we loved.
You thought you'd like another child. 'Too late,'

you said. And we fell silent, thought a while
of yours with his copper hair and mine,
a grown daughter and sons.

Then, that joke we shared, our phases of the moon.
'Sisterly lunacy' I said. You liked
the phrase. It became ours. Different

as earth and air, yet in one trace that week
we towed the calends like boats reining
the oceans of the world at the full moon.

Suddenly from the fields we heard again
a baby cry, and standing at the door
listened for minutes, eyes and ears soon used

to the night. It was cold. In the east
the river made a breath of shining sound.
The cattle in the field were shadow black.

A cow coughed. Some slept, and some pulled grass.
I could smell blossom from the blackthorn
and see their thorny crowns against the sky.

And then again, a sharp cry from the hill.
'A hare' we said together, not speaking
of fox or trap that held it in a lock

of terrible darkness. Both admitted
next day to lying guilty hours awake
at the crying of the hare. You told me

of sleeping at last in the jaws of a bad dream.
"I saw all the suffering of the world
in a single moment. Then I heard

a voice say 'But this is nothing, nothing
to the mental pain'." I couldn't speak of it.
I thought about your dream as you lay ill.

In the last heavy nights before full moon,
when its face seems sorrowful and broken,
I look through binoculars. Its seas flower

like cloud over water, it wears its craters
like silver rings. Even in dying you
menstruated as a woman in health

considering to have a child or no.
When they hand me insults or little hurts
and I'm on fire with my arguments

at your great distance you can calm me still.
Your dream, my sleeplessness, the cattle
asleep under a full moon,

and out there
the dumb and stiffening body of the hare.

Llŷr

Ten years old, at my first Stratford play:
The river and the king with their Welsh names
Bore in the darkness of a summer night
Through interval and act and interval.
Swans moved double through glossy water
Gleaming with imponderable meanings.
Was it Gielgud on that occasion?
Or ample Laughton, crazily white-gowned,
Pillowed in wheatsheaves on a wooden cart,
Who taught the significance of little words?
All. Nothing. Fond. Ingratitude. Words
To keep me scared, awake at night. That old
Man's vanity and a daughter's 'Nothing',
Ran like a nursery rhythm in my head.

Thirty years later on the cliffs of Llŷn
I watch how Edgar's crows and choughs still measure
How high cliffs are, how thrown stones fall
Into history, how deeply the bruise
Spreads in the sea where the wave has broken.
The turf is stitched with tormentil and thrift,
Blue squill and bird bones, tiny shells, heartsease.
Yellowhammers sing like sparks in the gorse.

The landscape's marked with figures of old men:
The bearded sea; thin-boned, wind-bent trees;
Shepherd and labourer and night-fisherman.
Here and there among the crumbling farms
Are lit kitchen windows on distant hills,
And guilty daughters longing to be gone.

Night falls on Llŷn, on forefathers,
Old Celtic kings and the more recent dead,
Those we are still guilty about, flowers
Fade in jam jars on their graves; renewed
Refusals are heavy on our minds.
My head is full of sound, remembered speech,
Syllables, ideas just out of reach;
The close, looped sound of curlew and the far
Subsidiary roar, cadences shaped
By the long coast of the peninsula,
The continuous pentameter of the sea.
When I was ten a fool and a king sang
Rhymes about sorrow, and there I heard
That nothing is until it has a word.

Neighbours

That spring was late. We watched the sky
and studied charts for shouldering isobars.
Birds were late to pair. Crows drank from the lamb's eye.

Over Finland small birds fell: song-thrushes
steering north, smudged signatures on light,
migrating warblers, nightingales.

Wing-beats failed over fjords, each lung a sip of gall.
Children were warned of their dangerous beauty.
Milk was spilt in Poland. Each quarrel

the blowback from some old story,
a mouthful of bitter air from the Ukraine
brought by the wind out of its box of sorrows.

This spring a lamb sips caesium on a Welsh hill.
A child, lifting her face to drink the rain,
takes into her blood the poisoned arrow.

Now we are all neighbourly, each little town
in Europe twinned to Chernobyl, each heart
with the burnt fireman, the child on the Moscow train.

In the democracy of the virus and the toxin
we wait. We watch for bird migrations,
one bird returning with green in its voice,

glasnost,
golau glas,
a first break of blue.

(*golau glas* blue light)

Seal

When the milk-arrow stabs she comes
water-fluent down the long green miles.
Her milk leaks into the sea, blue
blossoming in an opal.

The pup lies patient in his cot of stone.
They meet with cries, caress as people do.
She lies down for his suckling, lifts him
with a flipper from the sea's reach
when the tide fills his throat with salt.

This is the fourteenth day. In two days
no bitch-head will break the brilliance
listening for baby-cries.
Down in the thunder of that other country
the bulls are calling and her uterus is empty.

Alone and hungering in his fallen shawl
he'll nuzzle the Atlantic and be gone.
If that day's still his moult will lie
a gleaming ring on sand
like the noose she slips on the sea.

from *Cofiant*

Thomas Williams (1800-1885)

Child of Christmas and the turning century,
born to holy bells and the tolling sea,
he carried two voices into manhood:
the call of the sea and the call of God.

He writes how he'd never known a time
when longing for sea's rhythm
underfoot and the hot rope in his hands
reining an apron of sail as he held the wind,

was not a stinging fire in his mind,
or when the tug of religion started
turning his heart into the gale.
He took lodgings in Pwllheli and set sail.

The boat carried limestone across the Straits,
Môn to Caernarfon. He set his sights
on the torn coastline, crossing the grain
of knotty currents, westerlies and rain.

*

He was baptised in the stream at Tyddyn Shôn.
I found the place one summer afternoon
where water twisted, as it must have done,
under the bridge in a pool deep enough for a man
to drown his devils in a mountain stream,
leaving his soul caught like a rag on a stone.

John Penri Williams (1899-1957)

In the margins of books, poems printed
on foxed, bevelled pages; under the shelf
where we peeled back the old wallpaper;
lists; old letters; diaries; notebooks;
copperplate in blacklead and washable Quink,
the Conway Stewart with a golden lever
and its intake of sound as the ink-sac swelled;
commentary; schedules; signatures.
How, after thirty years, do I know his hand?

Chapel boy from Carmarthenshire
locked in his cabin, writing home,
'Annwyl Mam,' shocked by crew-talk,
or tapping morse as the world burned.
He drummed bad news on the sea's skin,
his air-waves singing over the roof
of the whale's auditorium. Only his heart,
the coded pulse over dark water
to a listening ship and the girl at home.

Twenty years away his daughter waits
to knock him dizzy with her birth
and scarcely twenty more
he'll strike her silent with his death,
going out on a rainy evening
in May when she isn't looking,
with a 'Hwyl fawr, Cariad.'
No message. Just, 'Over'.

*

An over-turned wine-glass
in wet grass,
one sip like guilt
in the spoon of the tongue.

The fire's dissolved
to bird-bones.
A small lake shivers
in the deck-chair's lap.

From *Letter from a Far Country*

When least expected you catch
the eye of the enemy
looking coldly from the old world...
Here's a woman who ought to be
up to her wrists in marriage;
not content with the second hand
she is shaking the bracelets
from her arms. The sea circles
her ankles. Watch its knots loosen
from the delicate bones
of her feet, from the rope of foam
about a rock. The seal swims
in a collar of water
drawing the horizon in its wake.
And doubt breaks the perfect
white surface of the day.

About the tree in the middle
of the cornfield the loop of gold
is loose as water; as the love
we should bear one another.

When I rock the sea rocks. The moon
doesn't seem to be listening
invisible in a pale sky,
keeping a light hand on the rein.

Where is woman in this trinity?
The mare who draws the load?
The hand on the leather?
The cargo of wheat?

Watching sea-roads I feel
the tightening white currents,
am waterlogged, my time set
to the sea's town clock.
My cramps and drownings, energies,
desires draw the loaded net
of the tide over the stones.

A lap full of pebbles and then
light as a Coca Cola can.
I am freight. I am ship.
I cast ballast overboard.
The moon decides my Equinox.
At high tide I am leaving.

The women are leaving.
They are paying their taxes
and dues. Filling in their passports.
They are paying to Caesar
what is Caesar's, to God what is God's,
To Woman what is Man's.

I hear the dead grandmothers,
Mamgu from Ceredigion,
Nain from the North, all calling
their daughters down from the fields,
calling me in from the road.
They haul at the taut silk cords;
set us fetching eggs, feeding hens,
mixing rage with the family bread,
lock us to the elbows in soap suds.
Their sculleries and kitchens fill
with steam, sweetnesses, goosefeathers.

On the graves of my grandfathers
the stones, in their lichens and mosses,
record each one's importance.
Diaconydd. Trysorydd.
Pillars of their society.
Three times at chapel on Sundays.
They are in league with the moon
but as silently stony
as the simple names of their women.

We are hawks trained to return
to the lure from the circle's
far circumference. Children sing
that note that only we can hear.
The baby breaks the waters,
disorders the blood's tune, sets
each filament of the senses

wild. Its cry tugs at flesh, floods
its mother's milky fields.
Nightly in white moonlight I wake
from sleep one whole slow minute
before the hungry child
wondering what woke me.

School's out. The clocks strike four.
Today this letter goes unsigned,
unfinished, unposted.
When it is finished
I will post it from a far country.

Overheard in County Sligo

I married a man from County Roscommon
and I live at the back of beyond
with a field of cows and a yard of hens
and six white geese on the pond.

At my door's a square of yellow corn
caught up by its corners and shaken,
and the road runs down through the open gate
and freedom's there for the taking.

I had thought to work on the Abbey stage
or have my name in a book,
to see my thought on the printed page,
or still the crowd with a look.

But I turn to fold the breakfast cloth
and to polish the lustre and brass,
to order and dust the tumbled rooms
and find my face in the glass.

I ought to feel I'm a happy woman
for I lie in the lap of the land,
and I married a man from County Roscommon
and I live in the back of beyond.

TONY CURTIS

I write because it is easier than not writing. It makes sense. Poetry is the most effective way I know of recording, in a considered way, my ideas and experiences, and of introducing myself to myself. I am not talking about *confessional poetry*, I have written directly about myself on few occasions in the last ten years, and since then a number of poems dealing with my father's death. Through the 1980s, and now at the beginning of a new decade, I am working at the craft of a poetry that performs as interesting a role as fiction. I am speaking in new voices, other people's voices, and am attempting to create and re-create stories.

Why don't I write these ideas and experiences (albeit vicarious experiences) directly as short stories? Well, I have done that too, and may well turn to the short story again. It does, however, seem to be more compelling, more natural, for me to explore people and their situations through poetry at the moment. 'More natural'? How can poetry, that most wrought of the written arts, foregrounding as it does language in all its flashy, far-fetched manifestations, how can poetry be *natural*? Well, perhaps it is simply that it has become, for me, the obvious place to go with my thoughts, my ideas and the stories I've taken from others.

I realize that this fictive approach may well disturb and disappoint some readers. As we reach the end of the twentieth century I am aware that whatever audience there might still be for poetry retains expectations rooted in the nineteenth century. The legacy of the Romantics is still alive. Poets are sensitive beings, meditating or raging at the centre of a cruel or indifferent universe. Souls are to be bared, secrets recognized and shared. Frequent performers of their poetry (a practice which is, currently, the only sure way to make money as a poet) develop catch-phrases, witty off-the-cuff asides sprinkled like yeast to work the considered weight of their words. It is now my practice to say that I wish an audience to leave my reading knowing little more about me than when they entered. If I'm really trying to impress I throw out a reference to Keats and 'negative capability'. 'My life is boringly regular, but the world around is not,' I say. I cite Browning's wonderful dramatic monologues; pass on my enthusiasm for the contemporary American Norman Dubie. Like all acts, it is rehearsed and brittle, but until the next death, the next X-ray, the fresh pain, it will do.

Preparations

In the valley there is an order to these things:
Chapel suits and the morning shift called off.
She takes the bus to Pontypridd to buy black,
But the men alone proceed to the grave,
Neighbours, his butties, and the funeral regulars.
The women are left in the house; they bustle
Around the widow with a hushed, furious
Energy that keeps grief out of the hour.

She holds to the kitchen, concerned with sandwiches.
It is a ham-bone big as a man's arm and the meat
Folds over richly from her knife. A daughter sits
Watching butter swim in its dish before the fire.
The best china laid precisely across the new tablecloth:
They wait. They count the places over and over like a rosary.

Games with My Daughter

The first clear afternoon of Spring bursts
April's buds and bulbs in the park.
This year when I catch and take her weight
she powers the swing and arcs
from finger-stretch behind my head
to soaring feet-in-the-clouds.
Mothers to our left and right
shrink in their corridors of safe flight.

Our game's revealed the filling out,
the firmer, young woman's stare,
the promise Winter concealed beneath its coat.
Forward and up she splits the sky, each
swing down and back she goes by to where
my tip-toed fingers' grasp can't reach.

My Father in Pembrokeshire

One of those godly days on the Headland,
gorse with the yellow coming to burst,
the tight heather and curled grasses sprung underfoot.

Such days are numbered for you,
we spend our time here like wages.
Precious the slow, awkward breathing,
the laboured talk is precious.

The sand over on Caldey never seemed so bright,
the island stretching empty arms to the west
in that early summer Sunday
before the trade fills the streets and the beaches,
and the noise of the day washes
out from the town a mile or more,
louder than sea.

I have to go further down.
I have to go down to the water.
The way is worn and rough and safe;
I crawl to the edge of a chimney shaft.
The sea lies calm as well-water,
green with rocks growing patterns underneath.

To lose myself in the long moment,
drinking in the depth, the abstract shapes.

Back at the top, you say –
Feel my neck –
and the growths blossom along your throat
under my fingers.

Under the sun, the prodigal sky,
there are no healing waters.

Return to the Headland

There seems no point in angels
or ogres. Now I have no need
for the cartoons of guilt or shame.
The dead go where we send them.
At the crematorium I read 'Do Not Go Gentle'
before the vicar's book freed
your soul or whatever it be that soars
from the husk of flesh.
The curtains purred to their close.
Outside, the long summer of rain,
grey and grey and grey blurred
over Narberth's sodden hills.

It would be easy to construct a myth.
The box jammed under
the baby-seat in the back of the car,
bumping our way up to the Headland.
Early evening. The sea green and flat,
moving and murmuring in the hollows beneath
our feet. Not a cloud shaped, though the horizon
east across Wales is dimming into grey.
The urn is some sort of alloy
like a child's toy, light and wrapped around
what we're told are your ashes.

Not in the sea – says my mother –
he was never a man for the sea –
I step off the path to the slope of rocks
and two rabbits break for cover
from the startled grass.
The stuff shakes out and falls free:
dust, ash on the stones, my shoes.
Stiff-armed, I send the empty tin
over the edge right down to the water.

A jet chalks its line high above the ocean,
pushing steadily away from night.
We turn our backs on a sky that goes on for ever.

The Last Candles

The final stage of our journey over
we reached Odessa. So glorious
a scene I think my eyes had never taken in –
the harbour bristling with ships of all the allied nations.
We were received at the consulate by a young man,
fresh and clean in a crisp English suit.
Courteous and gentlemanly. I had not seen
such a man for four years.

In the hotel that night my dreams were of uniforms
and wounds, but one wound served for many –
thus, a severed arm at Biyech, the lacerated
stomach of a boy in Khutanova, the bloody head
of a captured Turk in Noscov – and then swabs
fell like the first snows of Winter,
the land chill and beyond pain
under its bandages.

For breakfast we were offered good bread and an egg.
The smell of coffee made me dizzy.

At nine we leave for the harbour. The streets
packed with aimless crowds, though everything
makes way for the *Bolsheviki* in their lorries.
At the harbour gates a man of no apparent rank
holds our papers for an hour.
He has a rifle and a long knife hangs
from his belt. A red band has been clumsily
sewn to the sleeve of his coat.

Some of the Norwegian crew speak English.
My cabin proves small, but warm.
After years under canvas, sheltering in ruins,
nursing beneath shattered roofs,
I am glad to call it home.
Though the place is strange and metallic
after stone and wood and earth.

Doctor Rakhil calls to take me on deck
for our departure.
                              Ten years of living in this great land

have brought me to love it.
Though three of those years have been spent in war,
and then this anarchy, this revolution.
I see Odessa under red flags
as we cast off and the engines churn.
I feel everything moving away from me
as if Russia were a carpet being rolled to the sky.
At the harbour mouth Doctor Rakhil
gently turns me from the rail,
but is not quite quick enough.

That night, the sea pressing around me,
I dream of three things –
                    a day
in Moscow, when Nadya and I
were close enough to reach out and touch
the Tsar, and an old peasant
who had crawled through the crowd, between
the legs of the guards, clutching
his ragged petition,
still calling out as their boots struck him.
Nicholas II, Tsar of all the Russias, flickered
his eyes, but his step was the unfaltering
step of a god.
                    My first dead man
in the training ward. Grey and small in the candlelight,
his mouth like a closed purse and what seemed
to be butterflies on his face. Two sugarlumps
to weigh down his eye-lids.

                    And at last, this leaving
Odessa. How in the shadows I saw them –
officers from the front fleeing the chaos of desertion
and caught by the Reds at the port.
They bound their feet to heavy stones
and planted them in the harbour. Swaying, grey shapes
I glimpsed from the rail, as if
bowing to me.
The last candles of my Russia
guttering and going out under the black sea.

The Death of Richard Beattie-Seaman in the Belgian Grand Prix, 1939

Trapped in the wreckage by his broken arm
he watched the flames flower from the front end.
So much pain – *Holy Jesus, let them get to me* –
so much pain he heard his screams like music
when he closed his eyes – the school organ at Rugby
Matins with light slanting down
hot and heady from the summer's high windows.
Pain – his trousers welded by flame to his legs.
His left hand tore off the clouded goggles –
rain falling like light into the heavy trees,
the track polished like a blade.
They would get to him, they were all coming
all running across the grass, he knew.

The fumes of a tuned Mercedes smelt like
boot polish and tear gas – coughing, his screams rising
high out of the cockpit – high
away back to '38 Die Nurburgring.
He flew in with Clara
banking and turning the Wessex through a slow circle
over the scene – sunlight flashing off the line of cars,
people waving, hoardings and loudspeakers, swastikas
and the flags of nations lifted in the wind he stirred.
She held his arm tightly, her eyes were closed.
He felt strong like the stretched wing of a bird,
the course mapped out below him.
That day Lang and Von Brauchitsch and Caracciola
all dropped out and he did it – won
in the fourth Mercedes before a crowd of half a million
– the champagne cup, the wreath around his neck,
An Englishman the toast of Germany
The camera caught him giving a Hitlergruss.

Waving arms, shouts and faces, a mosaic
laid up to this moment – La Source – tight – the hairpin
the trees – tight – La Source – keeping up the pace
Belgium – La Source hairpin too tight.

With the fire dying, the pain dying
the voices blurred beneath the cool licks of rain.
To be laid under the cool sheets of rain.
A quiet with, just perceptible, engines roaring
as at the start of a great race.

Soup

One night our block leader set a competition:
two bowls of soup to the best teller of a tale.
That whole evening the hut filled with words –
tales from the old countries
of wolves and children
potions and love-sick herders
stupid woodsmen and crafty villagers.
Apple-blossom snowed from blue skies,
orphans discovered themselves royal.
Tales of greed and heroes and cunning survival,
soldiers of the Empires, the Church, the Reich.

And when they turned to me
I could not speak,
sunk in the horror of that place,
my throat a corridor of bones, my eyes
and nostrils clogged with self-pity.
'Speak,' they said, 'everyone has a story to tell.'
And so I closed my eyes and said:
I have no hunger for your bowls of soup, you see
I have just risen from the Shabbat meal –
my father has filled our glasses with wine,
bread has been broken, the maid has served fish.
Grandfather has sung, tears in his eyes, the old songs.
My mother holds her glass by the stem, lifts
it to her mouth, the red glow reflecting on her throat.
I go to her side and she kisses me for bed.
My grandfather's kiss is rough and soft like an apricot.
The sheets on my bed are crisp and flat
like the leaves of a book . . .

I carried my prizes back to my bunk: one bowl
I hid, the other I stirred
and smelt a long time, so long
that it filled the cauldron of my head,
drowning a family of memories.

Summer in Bangkok

The second day he bought a wife
for his stay.
He kept her in his room and fucked
her all the ways he'd ever dreamed.
She was fed and kept
and smiled and answered his needs.

It was perfect, save that her English
was a dozen, broken sentences.

Some days he would go to see the city:
then she soaked herself clean in the bath,
she moved around the room trailing her hand
over polished wood, curtains, picture frames.
She lay on the bed he tied her to.

And in the final week he took the interior trek
– eight guys led into the hills
and poisonous snakes, bare-teeth monkeys.
They burned leeches from their arms and legs.
In the trees were men with guns and heroin eyes.
Their women were invisible, their children sold to the city.

Each night he shivered. They were locked
in by the massive dark, a wall of sounds.
Like children they went to piss in pairs.
The sky was small and reversed. He saw
no plough, no bear, no hunter.
The stars would not be read.

On the fourth day they struck the river and turned,
made bamboo rafts with poles and rode the white water
back to the coast, the skyscrapers, the wild taxis,
the silk, the child beggars, career amputees.

Halfway, they poled a long, slow curve and met
the heroin men on both banks, rifles raised
and aimed at them. Their guide spoke loudly
and quickly, his hands eloquent, then fevered,
the rest kept still on the bobbing water.
He gripped his pole tightly, all he could do,
so it stuck and trembled in the river bottom.
He had no words.

Back in the hotel she lay on his bed,
her hair spread wet on his pillow, her arms
and legs, as it were, swimming.

Home Front

That winter of our Island Fortress,
the docks blacked-out and sirens wailing,
the house closed its brittle silence around her.
Rain drummed the windows behind her children's dreams.
Over the months she saved from her widow's pay
and the hours of cleaning at the manse
seven silver coins, one from the abdication year
with the head of the love-lost king.

Should the coastline be split by incoming shells,
parachutes flower in the Vale
and jackboots strut in King's Square,
then she would lay her six children
to sleep, sealing the windows and doors
with newspapers and blankets.
Seven shillings' worth of gas
would deliver them out of occupation.

For months she has dreamt of his lost freighter,
torpedoed six days out of New York,
men overboard, gagging on salt and diesel.
How the ship reared and plunged like a whale,
her wash sweeping cold hands from flotsam.
As he sank into the anonymous dark
the final waves from her
minting coins from the constant moon.

Tonight the City of London burns
with St Paul's untouched at the very centre.
At the edge of night the Welsh ports sound no alarms.
She opens the curtains to a moon-bright sky,
counts out the coins in the tea-caddy
and holds them, cupped in her palms.
OMN. REX. *Defender of the Faith. Emperor of India.*
The seven polished shillings sing in her hands.

Friedhof

They are tending the dead at Ypres.
The beech leaves, November bronze,
are lifted and rolled over
into rows between the slabs
by the gardener's blower
while three others follow to rake
the long mound and fork
this harvest into their barrows.

Behind the barbs of squared beech hedge
each yard of peace names its German dead,
twenty by twenty on dark, flat slabs
so that, without the steady sweepers,
you might come to this place as to a park,
tread the leaves in a path to the two figures
– a man, a woman; a father, a mother,
kneeling sharp and hunched before
some undetermined loss.

Years after the war, Kathe Kollwitz,
finding at last her only son's grave,
shaped these two from stone.
Now, his wooden cross a museum piece,
his name is flattened with the others
under this brief quilt of leaves.

At Tyn Cot, The New Irish Farm,
St Julien Dressing Station,
at Sanctuary Woods, at Lijssenthoek,
and a hundred cemeteries more,
the victorious dead, white-stoned, upright,
are ranked in the democracy of death –
Dorset, Welch, Highlander, Sikh,
Six men of the Chinese Labour Force.
The whole world bled through Flanders.

Turning the wet earth, Flemish farmers
still find wire and bones
tangled with the potatoes and beet.
And, occasionally, the local paper
carries at the bottom of a page –
Farmer blinded by shell.
It happens when they remove the detonator
from the rusty casing. The trade is well
established. The explosive is tired
but has a pedigree right enough for the men
of Armagh, Fermanagh, Crossmaglen.

JOHN DAVIES

Flight Patterns

Rich came over from Seattle and after I'd shown him the estuary rippling with implications, its washed-up footprints, the lighthouse which used to juggle ships till its arms shrank, he asked where Dawley was. His father had given him an address and a name, Kath Stoker. 'Check her out if you're passing.' I'd met his father, Ed, on his small-holding the year before, a man of few words and several hundred ducks. He'd looked content, standing in the shadow of huge conifers where trailer homes conspired as small places seem to when you're passing through. Ed had built a life there. I'd felt nostalgic, going having measured what returning was for. When Rich had returned from the war in Vietnam, he'd found that his father's main customers were local Vietnamese to whom duck eggs, eaten raw, were a delicacy.

Ed had serviced fighters at the US airbase near Dawley during World War II. After it was all over, airmail letters started arriving which Rich's mother placed mid-table at breakfast but Ed would make no move. (Rich's uncle told him this.) Only the fire opened them.

I'd planned a trip to south Wales anyway, where I was brought up, so we just had to veer a few miles east of Shrewsbury to reach Dawley. First though we traced what remained of the airbase, directed by a garage mechanic who remembered two Thunderbolts colliding overhead. From an ordnance store deep in undergrowth and barbed wire, pigeons took off to reconnoitre cloud over a runway of furrows. Then we entered Dawley.

Rich described in a letter his arrival home. The first thing his father had said was to ask whether – ? Yes, said Rich, but no, nobody in New Street had heard of Kath. Dressed only in himself, Ed had turned on his heel, gone back to bed. And next day, among sheds like a railroad accident, he was tending ducks again with their clipped wings.

The story touches on themes I've been held by in recent years, two of them spent in Washington and Utah, the others in a small town on the north Wales coast. In particular, standing still and flying (or at least moving) suggest ways of being that are as compelling as they are mutually exclusive. The tension between them, two knots of values I can best approach through metaphor, is strong. But then if I believed that flying while standing still really was impossible – if I didn't live in Wales, itself a cloud changing and not changing to stay intact – I wouldn't be writing poetry.

Country

Roaming the airwaves again are rhinestone
cowgirls called Tammy, Loretta, Crystal,
with doomwails of steel guitars.
My wipers blink the blurred road
clear. Even the river nursed in its bed
by sympathetic branches lends an ear.

Heart-stomped, they're stranded
in love's garden. Why though pick late-flowering
philanderers? To be on their wavelength
I'd need me a Ford pickup and more.
Folk I was raised with kept their griefs
well under wraps, they had no truck
with breakdowns. Would they be leaning on hard
shoulders here, mourning the humped bridge?

But trying to switch off,
my arm does the hesitation waltz.
'Ease up,' soft tyres sigh.
'Let go, let go,' whisper wipers.

Hymns used to work for them. No road though
runs back, and anyway the songs
aren't all strife. Why not just sag along?
This one's all heart, listen, *Dropkick Me
Jesus Through the Goalposts of Life*.

From *The Visitor's Book*

Cymmer pays out road, it drifts apart.
I'd see him pass then later would learn why,
as a zealous Press damned all 'the workshy'
from high ground, that shrewd veteran Dr Hart
still sends his tall voice across country,
telling how hard at work are the strains
of virus stagnant waters breed where veins
of coal and promise dry up suddenly.

Gone are the flyaway young, the railway.
For the rest, by now all they have come to fit
is too much theirs to detach themselves from it.
Houses, hunched, small-shouldered, face the way
out. The good flat road stretches half-awake
from a life which it steeped whole lives to make.

*

Thanks to the street-lamp, nightly my bedroom
screens *Branches*, art on a low budget
restless for review. I give it small notice.
So why a stone-still place I barely know
has been showing in my head for days,
all valley gothic and November dusk,
I can't tell. My bronzed brother in America
has yanked such dankness out. At home
in foreign parts ('Shalom, you-all!'), his sights
locked on what's Now like an astronaut,
he cannot stand repeats. He's gone native
west of space. Are old workings still inhabited?
He couldn't give a damn. That's style. Just let
me run these streets through one more time...

The Bridge

Gareth, this photograph you sent
records August when we met again –
in a city this time like a rocket base.
White clusters judder at the sky.
Our vantage point's a spur of rock
and ahead a bridge, the Golden Gate,
takes off through floes of mist.

I was your second-in-command.
Talking, we watched all afternoon
quick ferry boats pay out the distances
that would always haul them back.
Now that you're at ease in sunlight west
of everywhere, roads you took
return east to Colorado then freeze up.

And we talked of another place,
the bleak hometown ten months before.
Rain rinsed the streets. Our father dead,
we'd gathered in an emptied house
to mourn new space between us all.
Comings, goings, made less sense.
Distance ahead blurred out the focus.

A year from now, ten years, let this bridge
still be there still strung firm
across flotations and coldwater miles,
this connection our father tightened
in a town of steel to show us
the meeting-point survives
and wherever we rediscover it is home.

Pursuit

I've been reading letters my father sent
after D-Day, the edging inland
through Normandy under fire from mosquitoes
then rain, sleep chopped in fragments
('all the guns in France won't wake me')
and, after stand-to, breakfast canned.

'We have come back from the front.' Censored,
stray shellfire bursts through anyhow.
A lot's buried. He bathed 'in our English Channel',
sang *Lledrod* in an apple orchard.
I'd ask if Collinge made it, Smith,
but all those guns wouldn't wake him now

and at least one risk made him blunt:
the abbey at Mont St Michel 'is treacherous
without a guide. There are secret passages
so one can easily get lost.' *About the front* ...
I'd have probed, though we are too slow
to ask the past much, slipping from us.

Still turning the dark side from his family,
he stored the letters in this book he'd keep
safe. He knew us, I think. We hardly knew
the half of him. What he let us see
was the orchard in him, light cover, you'd
have to guess the dugout seven feet deep,

and I know now that when we let
silence speak it didn't, would not
speak for us, marching to the old tune
Sons and Fathers that we couldn't forget.
So looking at my daughter
suddenly I need to say something but what.

Freedom Boulevard

My daughter talked namebrand jeans, the Mall,
as we left the city on 200 West that became one day
without a blush, Freedom Boulevard. Bulging in heat,
cars wobbled like toads. Each day she chants in class,
'I pledge allegiance to the flag of the United States...'

The road racing straight ahead, uncoiling sun,
braked in the mining district. You climb past Ephraim
into Wales from the east and it's small,
dry ground's shrunk to a litter of bleached jobs.
Turkey sheds glared into gaps left unexplained.
At the tiny post office, when Mary Davis scanning
my postcard asked if that's Welsh, 'No, that's
my writing,' I said. Keep Off signs peppered testily
with buckshot said connection is accident, that's all.

Sight's longer in dry air: weightless, we fell
like stones on distance whose ripplings
smoothed themselves to a circle with no edges,
the one target that proves anyone's aim true.

The drive-in had *Snow White*. Desert had the darkness,
even the flagged principalities of car dealerships.
Our block squared its shoulders where the garage
yawned surprise – isn't the point of travel to keep
going? – then shut up.

Farmland

Inland from the English-speaking sea,
where I lose my bearings and my wife translates,
market towns gather villages.
Henllan, Trefnant, Llanrhaeadr had come
past trees brushing mist from the fields
to Denbigh's plantation of telegraph poles.

Steps stood up, and high arched doors
checking again familiar faces
narrowly took me in. On her aunt's
coffin, flowers had drained the light
but not those packed pews: murmurs, ripples
were refilling farmland's hollows.

The minister's shock of eyebrows
hedging raw cheeks, he'd have hauled a ram.
Speech shook me off. It was tenors
gliding on familiar foreign words in search
of thermals drew me towards the woman
gone, to Joe who doesn't speak Welsh

or often, relying on closed ranks.
Once connection tunes its instruments,
feeling's airborne over fact
and, soaring, forgets it still bears
language asserting difference, how else
leap snags of common ground?

At the coast were fingers of cloud
all bruises and gold rings. Caravans
made one thin road an anywhere.

What we travel from also moves from us,
and gulls guarding clutches of pebbles
turned into people briefly then flew off.

Regrouping

As a boy Joe Washington had cigarettes
stubbed on his tongue. Now an old man
at the pow-wow downtown, he speaks
in the common currency. But sings in Salish.
Each winter the river floods his shack.
Winter again, language of willows pours
downstream on his niece dead, loss
greening loss till sharing sings him home
and the drumming starts, the dancing.

I go outside to smoke.
'We gave tobacco, the whites whisky.
Lung for a liver – fair exchange.'
The thrum of hunched drummers is wiped out
by trucks like warehouses sliding east.

Between dances a cop keeps raiding
the microphone. No drinking, check
your children. Holds up a knife he's found.
The watchers, passive or impassive, watch
and I think of a plane crash, survivors
of flung seats, stunned, who keep regrouping.

This singing in another tongue old anthems
in a shared redoubt, I've no part in.
But am not apart. I have been here before
elsewhere, just visiting from a century
aging faster than time that has said no
to so much now there's just money,
as though inside might be someone or
something I'd half-known and lost.

On a portrait by Kyffin Williams

A country near-slouch has spread
his knees. In the background
gone blank, a tousled shadow lives.
And somewhere a shadow jet, gorse
its escort of yellow pennants.

Though the chin has rounded on
its youth, like water he could get
up and stretch and walk across country.
High in the drowned valley,
conifers meet mirror selves.

His brown face weather-veined,
ready to answer, gleams
for a self not yet rubbed smooth –
somewhere he'd know, burnt roofs send up
the price of occupation.

Eyes aren't sure what they feel
about this. Such hair though,
it must take shears to tame. One hand
clamps a knee to earth, the other
lifts like a big black cup his busby.

The hall is still tonight.
He is at ease but not wholly
perhaps, Corporal Pritchard, Goat Major,
in red and gold, the uniform
weight of our country's two colours.

Swifts

Staying, moving. Both versions
claim the coast, illusions

of choice steep
depths here and beyond keep

prompting: packed in redoubts,
hiders watch runners wearing out.

Our hill, to us a giant cast
in rock, eyes at sea sail past.

But nowhere special's lee
is also where ships are mostly,

and although smudged by tides
here is a lifetime wide.

Sometimes staring at Where again
eases the strain

of Who, looking out there's
safer. Though a lot of who is where.

What's sure is: not enough alive,
waking, I try

to keep in sight
one-off airy sleights

of place as they somehow
light up here and now.

I've inherited what I fit
almost, tried living in not on it.

Still, out there's blur
is mostly the one in here.

Look at swifts, spun
arcs bounced off reflections

of themselves in a rippled place
towards definition none trace

yet seem to aim for, stirred by flares
on water. Thirst here, now, everywhere.

In the absence of belief,
connect sun, look, with that leaf.

And there are sounds
always voicing familiar ground.

Just out of sight, human shapes
are reclaiming wired landscapes:

what's past too
prompts Where's conspiracy with Who,

and should being British strike a chord
I'll know I am abroad

where (though distance lends detachment,
little else is lent)

anyone can go, the knack
is in getting back,

Elsewhere-at-Home no nearer, the one
impossible destination.

CHRISTINE EVANS

I started writing suddenly in 1979, perhaps in reaction to the non-verbalizing way I was living, at home on a small-holding with infant son and fisherman husband in a small community that is one of the last toe-holds of a traditional culture. I was struck most by its patterns, the invisible web of relationships and deferential conventions that held the community together, and the way it remains a relatively frugal way of life, crofting rather than farming, on a handful of small, salt-scorched fields. There are more incomers now, and a high proportion of elderly residents, but young people are resisting the need to move away, and Uwchmynydd has kept its Welsh character.

'Callers' and 'Part Timer' represent the first poems I wrote within this context. My aim was to be plain, and while avoiding a romantic view, redress the balance a little by showing some of the joy, humour and satisfactions of 'peasant' culture. Though more overtly personal, 'Mynnydd Rhiw' also employs the idea of a secure pattern in contrast to the sense of exposure that is a feature of living at the extreme of a peninsula. The 'mountain' is less than 900 feet but being so close to the sea gives an exaggerated sense of height.

'Second Language' and 'Small Rain' are about lessons with sixth-formers. It is quite usual for a few pupils to excel at A level in both their languages, but the first poem explores my sense of guilt at succeeding in making them see English as a more attractive medium for personal expression at a time when the Welsh syllabus was still rather starchy and academic. In the Chernobyl poem, I like the contrast between the small contained classroom and what's happening on the surface of the mind with the wider perspectives that suddenly force themselves into focus. It works much better that none of the male pupils were present, becoming a poem about fertility.

A line in Section VI of 'Cometary Phases' sums up the two worlds, academic and practical, that my son is heir to, working on his own future 'Between *Hamlet* and *The Seaman's Book of Knots*'. It is a long poem in seven sections, each springing from attempts to catch a sighting of Halley's Comet in 1986, and addressed to my son who was determined to see it 'next time round', working out that he'd be 87. It concerns mortality and 'progress', the uncertain future and so on, but realized hopefully by domestic detail – so that above all, it becomes a poem about family. 'Enlli' was written for the daughter of a friend, to try and convey in simple language the calm and exhilaration I find on the island, Bardsey in English (or Norse.) It is the first poem, almost a preface, in the book I am working on, in which I am trying to use different forms in a succession of narrative voices.

Callers

It is always a shock when they take off their caps,
Those neighbouring farmers who call at our house.
They have to, of course, to have something to roll
Or to press or to twist in their blunt, nervous hands;
But it makes them instantly vulnerable
With their soft bald spots or thinning forelocks.
They seem at once smaller, and much more vivid:
Leaping out of type to personality.

The smell of their beasts comes in with them,
Faint as the breath of growing things in summer,
Rich, as the days draw in, with cake and hay and dung.
They are ill at ease in the house:
One feels they would like to stamp and snort,
Looking sideways, but have been trained out of it –
As with leaving mucky boots beside the door.

Only small, swarthy men with the friendly smell on them;
Yet walls press close and the room seems cluttered.
I am glad to go and make obligatory tea
As their voices sway, slow with the seasons,
And, ponderously, come to the point.

Part Timer

Yes, he says, he has
A few pots out from Porth.
Does not explain how from the earliest days
Out fishing with his father and an uncle
It was a refuge from the day's repeated toil:
A different dimension.

    For one thing, no women,
With their nagging at his conscience, or his senses.
Only exhilaration and the early morning air
Rinsing the closeness of the cowpen from his clothes,
Stirring old sediment
Beneath the bother in his brain.

Now, like a drug,
It draws him more and more.
His eyes are always out beyond the islands,
Sharpening their blue with distance.
He leaves his cows hock-deep in dung
And lets the barley stand;
Fends off his wife to creep out in the dawn
And lingers on the beach
To come home with the tide.

The lobster cash
Is handy, he will say;
The visitors are always asking for a crab.
And – with diffidence – I don't mind
Going out, I like the fishing all right, too.

Mynydd Rhiw

'Higher,' Taid would urge,
Forking more loose hay up to a load
Precarious already. 'Lots of room
Above, you'll never bang your head.'

And now I see his point, though
Perching on this cairn feels much the same
Pressed close by an exhilarating blue
That, later, will be sharp with stars,

For the island where those hectic summers wer
Is dwindled to a daffodil bulb
Half-buried by the dark – a world
Contained as the intensities of childhood.

From up here we see it all
As the hawk does or the fighter pilot
Swooping the undulations
To rehearse a kill; grief or joy or goodness

Absolving into pattern
That like a well-made poem, will seem
The only version. Just to be here
Shrinks us into where, not who, we are:

Out on a limb,
At the extremity of a digit,
Poised on a ridge in a fingernail –
We grow dizzy at the scale of things.

We must go down.
The small places that we fill
Are waiting. It is not easy for my kind
To be detached, to stand up high.

Fodder

The first winter that my sister had no work
She kept a twist of meadow hay
To hand, she missed her beasts so much.

I recoiled when she thrust it at me from a pocket.
– *Here, smell this! Doesn't it remind you*
Of cow's breath on a frosty morning, milking?

The gesture was a flicker of her childhood.
(Small corpses, shells, a living slow-worm once.)
Another lorry rumbled past the rented basement room.

It looks like scratchings from an old birds' nest,
But peering close I saw no grey at all;
It was the steady gold of late sun shafting down

From chapel windows or a thundercloud
With strands of green that had come through
Their three-day cure to mineral calm.

Timothy and ryegrass, stems with windshine on,
Seedheads like kittens' tails, and clover
Crumbling into tea – a still and breathing sweetness

Made me remember her excited over textbooks
Teaching me the names of all the grasses
And coumarin, that rocks the fields to sleep

In June. For me, pulled threads of summer
A bracelet of bright hair
From afternoons gone cold. For her

Fodder, as good as you might find
For milk, or meat, or keeping sense
Alive. Within my hand, a small warmth grew.

Second Language

For Carys P., Carys T., Elena, Manon, Nia and Teyrnon

I watch their faces rise to meet me
from the green depths of a culture
older than I can fathom. They glide
as if weighted by dreams or water

through my lessons, taking notes,
assiduously handing in assignments
in good time, browsing gravely
through all the books I offer, *thanking* me –

and all the time I feel I could be
beguiling selkie people to the land
to the bright amnesiac desert air
where I burn off my life without blossoming.

Five girls and a boy riding a name out of myth
whose language fills the mouth like fruit
who have grown in the delicate light
of an old walled garden that was once the world.

Manon, whom I see in jet and amber
accepting tribute, was the first
tangled in the word-lures, drawn out
to stand beside me with her colours brittling.

She claims she heard no echoes, never sang
in her own language. Now the others hover
offering in devout, tentative palms
iridescence from the inside of their minds.

In their calm faces I can find no clues
that they are still at ease in their own skins
that dredging for this voice has drowned no other
and my teaching has not made them strangers.

Small Rain

May 1986: after Chernobyl

For weeks the wind strained from the east
So ground and air were dry with a touch of steel
the sky's face pursed, indomitable, blank.

Close in the pod of our own concerns
we have reached the nunnery scene
when the first rain sighs and draws our gaze.

I remember teaching them rain-as-symbol:
fertility, wholeness, healing, grace.
Larkin's arrow-shower. Heart's-ease of tears.

This falls so gently on dust-stiffened green
new leaves and blossom that we've waited for
we open windows to its breath – and hear

a million small mouths suck and whisper.

*I used to dream of dancing in the rain
with nothing on*, Rhiannon confides,
and no one titters, we nod and understand

a dozen women, eleven with their lives
unfolding, held still and curious as cattle
by rain in Wales! We gaze and go on gazing

as though not one of us had realized
the world could go on glistening
poisoned. The lesson falters; goes on

but I am seeing each of these grave girls
as a kind of ark, and Ararat
a point in time we have to hope to find

and listening to our futures being fed.

From *Cometary Phases*

IV
January: mist drifts over
the fields, deepening like water.
Twelve years ago tonight
caught up in a swirl
stronger than the moving tides
of sea or air, mere hundred-fathom-stirrers
we brought each other
to an unknown shore.

Sometimes still I see your arms jerk out
to clutch the emptiness
not knowing yet they're not
firm-muscled wings or fins.

Then the first cry: the commitment.

It is frighteningly easy to picture our children
bald-gummed, big-headed as the babies
they sprang out of. I see you
wrinkling back towards the knowledge
that looked out at me
through your newborn eyes:
a wisdom I could not have given you
a darker inkling, quieter,
more accepting of empty spaces
than you could have sucked from me
(unless in my turn I'll remember).

It was only later
you focused on yourself enough to cry
for the little comfort
flesh can offer. At first
a dry night rasping, a constrained stridor
scraped from you where you lay
carefully put
in your carefully-tended cot
(always grizzling against sleep
the wiping-out you craved and hated)
rising to a red-faced wet despair
clinging to the bars. And when I hummed
old tunes that soothed my baby sister
something in them spiked your grief
to howling.

Now you like it
when the light has gone
and shapes become provisional –
drawn outward on a great dark ship
you tell me as I look in on my way to bed
and find you wide-eyed with the curtains back
gazing at the frosty stars, that emptiness
of old exploding suns that makes you feel
There's something out there,
not just wastes. And, *Can we,* you used to ask
go out exploring in the middle of the night?
But when two years ago I woke you
after midnight in mild summer
and walked with you
between the breathing humps of bracken
up Pen Cristin, we were both
hushed, half-afraid
as of disturbing something rarer-nesting and more hesitant
than ordinary dark.

(Watch an infant, any two-year-old
dribbling paint, dabbling a hand
in the bathwater, letting
a pattern grow: drawing the spirals
a shell obeys, or a moth to the flame
drawing the shape of the galaxies

a swirl that links
each drop of seawater, each stone
with every star.
There must be more than one focus.)

Once, we made a game
of listing brightnesses
until they seemed too many to be counted.
I remember telling you
your first word – *golau*, Welsh for
light; at once, savouring its consonants
like falling ash, like owl feathers
you tried *tywyllwch*
as a fitting last.

tywyllwch: darkness

Being Fruit

We start off more like fruit than anything:
Look at Leonardo's drawings
The womb split open like a green horse-chestnut
Ridged and rinded, pomegranate-tough
Not seeming tearable as tissue paper
As vets will warn at lambing courses.
Injecting oranges feels just like flesh.

I know how fruit is harvested.
Each year I make a tiny ceremony
Cupping my hand to each apple and testing
(Hardly more than easing its weight)
Whether it has sucked enough
Is full of sweetness enough
To let go. Then I settle each one
In a nest of waxed paper
And close the curtains against winter.

We end up parked in a bed
With a bag of guts and a stubborn bone-bundle
White light staring us out
And wrists ready labelled.

The last words my mother found to say
Shoving us off in a lucid surge
This is the final indignity
Because we had to find a nurse to ask
If she could have her teeth in
So she turned her face
Away from us all
And, crossly, died. There is something in that:
Some cussed strength we might all wish for
To pinch out the quick
Of our own aching.

That's how I thought she'd done it for my dad
And yet his blood goes whispering in my cells
Remember that we mark the ground
With all we've been, both what we meant
To store or spill.... Let someone feel
They made it easy, that it was
Somehow a harvesting.

Enlli

for Ceri, when she was ten

We get to it through troughs and rainbows
falling and flying
rocked in an eggshell
over drowned mountain ranges.

The island swings towards us, slowly.

We slide in on an oiled keel.
Step ashore with birth-wet, wind-red faces
wiping the salt from our eyes
and notice suddenly

welling quiet, and how here the breeze
lets smells of growing things
settle and grow warm, like butterflies
drowsing, too fine-winged to see.

A green track, lined with meadowsweet.
Stone houses, ramparts to the weather.
Small fields that will run all one way
to the sea, inviting feet
to make new paths to their own
discovered places.

After supper, lamplight
soft as the sheen of buttercups
and a blossoming of candle-shadow
bold on the bedroom wall.

Outside, a swirl of black and silver.
The lighthouse swings its white bird round
as if one day it will let go
the string, and let
the loosed light fly
back to its roost with the calling stars.

PETER FINCH

Why these choices? 'A Welsh Wordscape' represents my earliest work, written at the time I first came into contact with Anglo-Welshness in full flood. It starts with a line borrowed from R.S. Thomas although as a poem it is completely my own. Most of my work between then, the late 1960s, and now, has involved experimenting with form. Fired by an almost permanent dissatisfaction with the methods of my fellow-poets, I have systematically ransacked modernism, trying out all its techniques and then adding a few of my own.

Poets who habitually get up on stage and make noises ('The Gripvac') or construct their poems out of found material ('The Computer's First Proverbs') tend to be misunderstood. The argument always seems to come down to definitions of poetry. Because what you do is not really like what everybody else does then it is suspect. 'It is awfully hard for anyone to / go on doing anything because / everyone is troubled by everything' to quote Gertrude Stein as re-arranged by myself. If only we could get away from our obsession about what constitutes poetry then we might enjoy ourselves a little more.

My work in performance – that is standing on stage, often accompanied by various props, declaiming to an audience there more for entertainment than art – has led to changes in the way I compose. My piece 'Hills', which again dips into R.S. Thomas, probably looks a little slow on the page but when performed its comments on the fickleness of South Walians and the fate of the Welsh language have a more ready impact. The same can be said for the extract from 'Soft Dada' included here. This is a concrete poem composed in true dada fashion for stage interpretation by voice, loud hailer and twirled tumble-drier tube. But outside that arena it still has a life on the page.

Despite constant searching for new ways of doing it, I still find myself reverting to traditional forms. 'Little Mag' tells the story of my days as editor of *Second Aeon*. 'Severn Estuary ABC' – less traditional and slightly overtaken now by events – still has a point to make. 'The Tattoo' is a piece of simple nostalgia.

Wales, of course, remains a permanent undercurrent to almost everything I do. It was not always but it has become so. Roland Mathias in his introduction to *Green Horse*, an anthology of young poets from Wales which Meic Stephens and I edited in 1978, suggested that in the future writing from Wales would become increasingly less Welsh. However much this may be the case for others, for me the opposite seems to be true.

From *A Welsh Wordscape*

1. To live in Wales,

    Is to be mumbled at
    by re-incarnations of Dylan Thomas
    in numerous diverse disguises.

Is to be mown down
by the same words
at least six times a week.

Is to be bored
by Welsh visionaries
with wild hair and grey suits.

Is to be told
of the incredible agony
of an exile
that can be at most
a day's travel away.

And the sheep, the sheep,
the bloody flea-bitten Welsh sheep,
chased over the same hills
by a thousand poetic phrases
all saying the same things.

To live in Wales
is to love sheep
and to be afraid
of dragons.

The Computer's First Proverbs

after Edwin Morgan

You can take a dog to the keyside, but you can't push him in
all is wet that starts to bark
if you pay peanuts you get them planted in the park
nothing should be done in haste but grip your trout
if you want fish, you must prepare for stink
he who fishes with the piper barks like a dog
he who fishes a tiger is afraid to wink
fish will out, fish will out
all roaring is the same in the dark

A dog in the brook is worth avoiding
think of a fountain and you froth in the head
speech is water, fish are water
it is too late to rub in embrocation after the dream has gone
strike while the law is out
put the stout dog to a deaf oven
flush the fridge if you have a long arm
idle lips make the best smoke rings
fishmongers always make room
it is all melted than ends melted
in May let the plugs bloom
You cannot roar with the workers and ignore the phone
it takes three waders to make a wet man
the longest dog winks all the way home

The Gripvac

a plack attack at it turk ticker
a pluk rattle at dip murk ricker
a plock riddle ta doop mook flicker
a plick robble at dop much ricker
a prick rubble ta dap mutt rocher
at prock hobble ta pap must roofer
at pratt rattle toe dap muck woofer
ex rat alltip et dip mick wuttle
ex rit alltat add dup mock wurtle
ex prit all tit sad dap mock tittle
ex plit all tot sud dap mock toggle
ex plain all tot sid ter mock tuttle
ex plain all that sid er mock turtle
explain all that said the mock turtle
explain all that said the mock turtle
explain all that said the mock turtle

no time
not now
nof nof
the avenues
first the avenues
first the avenues
first the tone

The following tone is a reference tone
recorded at our operating level:–

ex prit all tit
ex plit all tat
                sad dap
                mock toggle
plack attack attack attack aticker turk
grip attack avenues implac top none
assap grif arak impac none troon
advark arkak no no gryphon tone
allvik arkup no gryphon no pattertone tone
no gripturk afan arkvac no avenues no phone
no first, gripvac
no arkvenues
no phone

no no,
the avenues
first
said the gryphon
                graf graf
                implic implacable
                impatient tone
expit plick plissed, I insist.

adventures
no explana no ventre
no plainer no vexture
no planations no explension
no veturations no vexations
no extra nations
no explanation.
no explanation
duck,

said the gripvac,
no explanation,
these adventures
take
much less time.

   'Explain all that,' said the Mock Turtle.
   'No, no! The adventures first,' said the Gryphon in an impatient tone:
'Explanations take such a dreadful time.'
                           – Lewis Carroll

The Tattoo

At the ferro-concrete bike sheds
I pass a love-note to Veronica.
I wear long trousers and brylcream now
but her only interest is proven prowess.
I tattoo her name on my arm in Quink
with a penknife and show her.
She is unimpressed.
She goes out with a big ted from the fifth
who pisses over bog doors when you're in there.
He wears knuckle-dusters and can make a noise like a fart
with his armpit. Everyone is scared.
At break the Head tells me
that only criminals and soldiers sport tattoos
and sends me home to remove it.
My mother refuses. There is a dispute.
Magnificently my photograph
appears in the paper. Schoolboy Banned.
Our family are resolute.

It is over when by mistake
I wash a week later
and the whole thing goes.
I return to school a hero
where after assembly Veronica smiles
and the big ted breaks my nose.

Out At The Edge

Pembrokeshire Coast Path in winter

The wind comes in off the sea at Nolton
filling the Mariner's car park with sand.
There are no cars.
At the tide edge a lone tripper
throws pebbles through the drizzle.
I watch, dripping, with two ducks
and a chicken,
from the bottom of a barren hedge.
When I climb the track
towards Druidstone I leave bootmarks
like fossils in the fluid mud.
Why do it?
Beauty, light, passion.
Who knows.
I get the feeling that if there is
an edge to this world then it is here.
From the headland I stare out at America
but don't see it.
Mist, distance, earth's curvature,
or maybe it just isn't there.

Little Mag

Spend three hours
addressing envelopes.
Bic exhausted.
Towards the finish
the hand finds itself
totally unable to complete the
tight circle of a letter o.

The mags go out like ack-ack.

In exchange I get misprints
highlighted, protest, left topher
off his name, no comma, word missing,

poems, two renewals, one cancellation,
a shaky essay on the work
of someone I've never heard of,
a pair of sandals, a dead fish.

At the post office I have a
deal where they stick the stamps
on and I pay.
'Too much bad language,'
says the supervisor with a hat
speaking to me as
if I were a martian.
'We have women here.'
I make a note.

In the pub I drink
to wash it all out of me
but the landlord's got
a new one can't wait.
It comes at me across the pump
handles like a singing telegram.
Crap can't tell him.
Have another pint I smile.
Pretty full I say.

Tomorrow the library
abuse in the bookstores
rain.
A bag of post like a
sack of kippers.

Dear Editor
I enclose 38 poems about love.
My friends say these
are better than anything
else they've read.
I would like to buy your
magazine please send a
free copy.
I will pay for one
when I'm in it.

I enclose
Here are
I am sending
Please find
I submit
Could you
Will you
Please
It is important that
I hope
I must
I have to
I'm the best
I don't bother usually
but these poems of mine are
so well put together that I
read them twice after
writing them.

You are the way
You are the path
You are the light
You are the last beacon
in this verbal wilderness

I have faith
Help me

But I cannot.
Poetry is short on miracles.
I send a rejection

instead.

Hills

Just an ordinary man of the bald Welsh hills,
docking sheep, penning a gap of cloud.
Just a bald man of the ordinary hills,
Welsh sheep gaps, docking pens, cloud shrouds.
Just a man, ordinary, Welsh doctor, pen weaver,
cloud gap, sheep sailor, hills.
Just a sharp shard, hill weaver, bald sheep,
pilot pen rider, gap doctor, cloud.
Just a shop, sheer hill weaver, slate,
balder, dock gap, pen and Welsh rider.
Just slate shop, hill balder, docking,
shop gap, Welsh man, cloud pen.
Just shops, slate, docks, bald sheep,
Welsh idea, gutteral hills, ordinary cloud.
Just grass gap, bald gap, garp grap,
gap shot, sheep slate, gap grap.

       garp gap
       gop gap
       sharp grap shop shap
       sheeeep sugar sha
       shower shope sheep
       shear shoe slap sap
       grasp gap gosp gap
       grip gap grasp gap
       guest gap grat gap
       gwint gap grog gap
       growd gap gost gap
       gap gap gwin gap
       gap gop gwell gap
       gap gop gap gap
       gap gap gog gap
       gap gap gorp gap
       gap gap gap gap
       gap gap gap gap
       gap gap gap gap
       gap gap gap gap
       gap gap gap
immigrant slate mirth grot gap,
bald grass, rock gap, shot gap,
old Welsh shot gap, rumble easy,
old gold gap, non-essential waste gap,

rock docker, slow slate gap, empty rocker
rate payer, waste gap, cloud hater,
grasper balder, pay my money, dead,
trout shout, slate waste. language nobody
uses, bald sounds, sends, no one pens,
fire gap, failed gasps,
dock waste, holiday grey gap,
hounds, homes, plus fours, grip sheep,
four-wheeled Rover. Why not? Soft price,
Grown gravel, swift sais.
The problem gaps, ordinary television,
nationalist garbage, insulting ignorance,
shot sheep, uninvited bald interference,
don't need real sheep where we are,
sheepless, sheepless, Welsh as you are, still,
no gasps, gogs or gaps for us,
no,
point our aerials at the Mendip Hills.

From *Soft Dada*

Severn Estuary ABC

A is a hat. Sun on my head.
B binoculars I'm using
C across the water. Largest concentration.
D is design. Planned.
E in Europe. Believe that.
F is mud flats, wading birds
G for godwit, green sandpiper, grey plover
H is heavy population, heavy water.
I'm informed. I watch tv. My hat is
Just there to stop the sun burning.
Know what does it?
L is little suns in bottles. Heat.
M is the mighty atom.
N for no trouble in Oldbury, Hinkley Point, Berkley.
Old stuff, I know. They're not sure.
P soup of a public explanation.
Quantity before quality. The fuel of the future.
R is rich someone's salting somewhere. There's always someone.
Severn seeped solid. Sold down the river.
T is truth. Piece of fiction.
Ah yes.
U is understanding. It's safe.
V is very safe. Formation of ducks. Skinhead. Thatcher.
We buy it.
X marks the spot. The insidious ingress. The cancer.
Why don't we do something?
Z is the sound of us listening.

CATHERINE FISHER

Looking at this selection of poems I can see that they reflect many personally important images; those words and symbols that gradually assume an almost sacramental value, both for their inherent meanings, and for their mass of associations and resonances. Why do certain images rise so prominently in the imagination? At the moment mine seem to include voyages and islands, indeed the sea in general; that rich, draughty medieval chamber of stained-glass, tapestry and illuminated books; ice; cold weather, and sometimes, trees.

The subjects of the poems are representative; some are about Gwent, especially the country of the Severn, about spiritual journeys, or people and incidents from the past that have caught my interest. Some are about myths, those tantalizingly significant 'things that are told.'

I have also tried to include poems that experiment with forms and shapes – couplets, terza rima, triplets – some of which use rhyme, or rather a form of half-rhyme.

The poems have various sources. 'Immrama' draws on the fantastic voyages of Mael Duin, Bran, Brendan and the Celtic saints; that tradition of sailing on to whatever lies at the world's end, which has lingered into Gulliver and much modern science fiction. I enjoy the clarity of these stories, their rich colour and unexplained magic. The two 'Apostle Window' poems are part of a series of twelve, based on a largely imaginary set of windows, and 'Incident at Conwy' sprang from a footnote in a guide to Conwy Castle.

The Noah sequence is perhaps the most ambitious of the poems here. It seeks to re-tell, or rather to re-express, the myth of the Flood in various modern guises, and to say something about its significance for us. It seems to me that the story of Noah is an apt one for a society increasingly worried about ecological imbalance. Man's fate is still bound up with the animals; he is still on his ark, journeying through the emptiness to whatever awaits.

Severn Bore

Somewhere out there the sea has shrugged its shoulders.
Grey-green masses slip, rise, gather
to a ripple and a wave, purposeful, arrowing up
arteries of the land. Brown and sinuous, supple
as an otter, nosing upstream under the arching
bridge; past Chepstow, Lydney; Berkeley where a king
screamed; Westbury, where old men
click stopwatches with grins of satisfaction;
slopping into the wellingtons of watchers,
swamping the nests of coots, splashing binoculars.
And so to Minsterworth meadows where Ivor Gurney's ghost
walks in sunlight, unforgotten; past lost

lanes, cow-trodden banks, nudging the reeds,
lifting the lank waterweed,
flooding pills, backwaters, bobbing the floats
of fishermen, the undersides of leaves and boats,
and gliding, gliding over Cotswold's flawed
reflection, the sun swelling, the blue sky scored
with ripples, fish and dragonfly, stirred
by the drip and cloop of oars; and finally, unheard,
washing into the backstreets of the town to lie
at the foot of the high
cathedral; prostrate, breathless,
pilgrim from a far place;
refugee
from the ominous petulance of the sea.

Noah

1 Forty Days

This is the almost legendary hour.
Outside, the world dissolving;
around me the seeds of animals
sleep the cold sleep.

The fractious woman slumbers;
my restless boys, tight
in their dreams. Only
the old man listens.

I am frail flotsam; timbers
swollen on the tide.
It has been forty centuries
since I stood upright.

My craft is pitted, aimless,
arrival now not to be thought of;
stillness, no motion,
strange solidity underfoot.

I would be wary of such cessation;
if the movement should stop.
It was in silence
the voice spoke before.

Hearing it now would be wreckage,
splintered on a reef of sunlight,
the doors stove in by rainbows,
livestock cascading after my raven and dove.

2   Firmament

Slowly spinning, the probe descends.
This is the second he has sent;
Raven is lost.

He has no radio contact; in
this vacuum of dust and stars
cannot afford failure.

The blurred orb beneath him is untouched.
He carries the seed that will sow it,
garner its alien harvest.

Despite this, his mind looks back,
cannot forget the faces in the lost towns.
Because of that we chose him.

No world is new. Even this, rising
from its receding waters, is only the old,
washed, ready to try again.

3   Deluge

Today it rains roses and African violets,
purple spinning petals
piled about the wheelhouse and the deck
through this round window.
Forty days of gulls and meteorites
and water.

Tonight it rains acid on trees in Norway,
etching the windows of log-houses
with strange hieroglyphs,
unreadable for generations.
Forty days of runes and crystals,
and dead leaves.

In deserts it rains dust and locust,
the dry, desiccated itches
of skin and throat
flaking on the sun's anvil.
Forty days of thirst and blowflies,
and stones for bread.

Here it rains cats and dogs, frogs,
old women with sticks.
No portent would be missing
in a world's delirium.
Forty days of falling angels,
and a white dove.

4   Adrift

Drive them up to Pen-y-Bwlch
he said, the slow herd
with their chiming guide,
woolly with indirection.

When did the snow begin?
The glaze on my face is hours old,
these five sticks in the woollen glove
no longer mine.

Constriction round the heart,
ice in my beard; my mouth two
wooden slats warped and illfitting,
hammered askew.

I wear the white coat, the cold wool.
It lies unshearable on earth's shoulders;
my flock mites in the fleece, drowned
in the stiffened surge.

Body moulds this blue-white chamber,
bedded with animals, aching
bell silent. When did I last thrust the
dove of my hand to the air?

Drowsy, we wait the spade
shattering our crystal; the gasping
stars, the white astonished
world at our feet.

5   Ararat

I, Otto, write the last entry.
The forward shaft is flooded,
holed on rock. The sea

engulfs us. Schmidt is dead,
and the others, lost in the ruined city.
Perhaps I will see them yet.

I have just been down to the crew-deck; they
sit silent as beasts. Paulson said
they trust me. Me.

The order came, it had to be followed.
God knows, no-one wanted this journey,
me included.

I think of Anna's letter.
'After the turmoil, the calm sea.
Believe the future will be better.'

And now the future is here,
we must rise to meet it. We must open
the hatches. And we must surrender.

6   Rainbow

First the need for action,
world gone rotten.

Select one man,
mythical, but human.

Bring out the wooden vessel
to carry my Chosen;

load the future
on its cold timbers.

Stand back. Unleash the flood,
nails and blood,

darkness, carrion,
clouds on the sun.

Now the long endurance,
the body's penance;

deep burial in the stifling chamber.
My Chosen endures his winter.

Until the doors smash open, heart and eye;
angels roll back the sky

and look up, see my mark, my scar,
my bright stigmata!

St Tewdric's Well

Toad on the soft black tarmac knows it's there;
screened by deadnettle, tumbled with ivy.
He enters the water like a devotee,
annointed with bubbles.

If you lean over, your shadow shrouds him;
dimly your eyes find watersnails
down on the deep green masonry, and coins,
discarded haloes.

Tewdric's miracle, not even beautiful,
slowly effacing itself in exuberant nettles,
its only movement the slow clouds,
the sun's glinting ascension.

Lost in the swish of grasses, the hot road,
blown ladybirds, soft notes from a piano;
and over the houses the estuary grey as a mirror,
its islands stepping-stones for Bran or Arthur.

Immrama

First there was the island of the darkness.
When we rowed from there
the light was desolation for us.

And I remember a house with a golden chessboard
where we played too long.
What we lost I cannot remember.

As you go on it gets harder. Each landfall
an awakening of sorrows,
guile or treachery, the enticement of pleasures.

I lost my brother at the house of feathers,
good men at the harper's table.
There are always those who would hold us back;

you get used to the voices, the clinging fingers;
in every port the warning
'Beyond here is nothing but the sea.'

Islands of glass, islands of music and berries,
the isle of the locked door,
citadels and beaches where we dared not land,

these are behind us. Daily, the delirium rises;
it may be that smudge
on the horizon is a trick of my eyes.

And would we know that land if we should find it?
They say the scent of apples
wafts on the water; there is honey, hum of bees,

salmon leap into the boat. They say the others,
the lost ones, laugh on the sand.
But behind them, who are those strangers crowding the cliffs?

From *Apostle Windows*

John

In winter he runs on stars and a road of moonlight
That frosts the window underneath his feet;
Makes his young face haggard, his robe white.

And sometimes in the lamplight from the street
He races down the long dim afternoons
Through rain that soaks and darkens like a threat.

It is a long way to the tomb.
Too far for a man to run in isolation,
Hoping, not knowing, agitated by rumour and some

Desperate, quivering elation.
Through history he has run towards the dawn,
the grave-cloths cast aside, the implication.

Judas

Never in any church have I seen you;
never on windows or on squat misericords or carved
even in the dimmest, cobwebbed corner of a crypt;
and if I did, you would only be hanging,
clutching your silver ransom, offering
that treacherous kiss. They never have anything good
to say of you, and who can blame them?
Heretics are worse than unbelievers
in the eyes of the betrayed.
Still, I wonder how you would look, how they might
portray you – whether the beard would be swarthy,
the eyes shifty, aslant –
because there is a roundel here of Christ in Hell,
embracing a man waist-deep in fiery glass

whose medieval face turns up as if in shock.
The features of both are gone; scrubbed by history
to a blaze of sunlight, as if that moment
transcended all colour, all the
glazier's power to create.
Perhaps it is something in the kiss
that makes me wonder if they meant it to be you.

Marginalia: Iona

The wind pushes snow through the gap under the door;
ices each stalk of grass and marram.
On days like this the birds drop,
the vole flattens itself on the tunnel floor.

Fintan has taken to putting out crumbs,
stale bannocks – the grey geese scream for them.
Father Abbot wonders if such creatures have souls.
They both know the granary is empty.

Yesterday I dropped the golden cup,
my fingers were too numb.
Wine flooded the cracks on the floor.
Reverent, we lifted a cobweb of blood.

And sometimes at dusk when the candle flickers
the tapestries move.
Dogs and stag ripple and run
down the green hills of the fraying cloth.

The hound and the stag in the margins of my book
on paths of knotwork, under and over
chase the joyful, unending chase.
Carefully, I draw their gold threads.

They say Columba spoke with angels;
was once a prince in a warm house.
When he died his hands were blistered,
swollen with the ague and the world's rain.

The tide falls; at the fen's edge
it coats the stubble with ice like glass;
a new layer at each ebb, bubbled and gritty;
inside, the green blade, feeling no wind.

Incident at Conwy

During the Wars of the Roses a Lancastrian officer at Tal-y-Sarnau was shot by a marksman from the battlements of Conwy Castle. At this point the river is at least half a mile wide. The feat was recorded by several chroniclers.

1 Llewelyn of Nannau

Oh man, you are foolish to wear that surcoat.
The blue and the gold outrage the dull afternoon.
You are a heraldic flicker among the leaves,
tempting my pride.
I have not killed men in the stench and fury
of battle only, that I would baulk at this.
I am an archer. I send death winging,
sudden, and cold, over parapet and fosse;
the lightning that strikes nowhere twice.
I am too far away to see your pain;
the blood that will sully your bright coat.
Too far to hear the shriek from your lady's arbour.
Nor will imagination spoil my aim.
The taut string creaks against my fingers,
brushes my cheek softly, as I draw back.
My eye is steady down the shaven shaft.
You are a roebuck, a proud stag, a target.
Your words do not goad me, I cannot hear what you say.
Your death will be skillfully given, and without rancour.
At least I am not too far from you for that.

2 Rhys ap Gruffudd Goch

The river is wide, and the leaves cover us;
we are safe enough – but they are certainly ready.
Each tower and arrowslit is crowded with faces,

and notice the fool on the battlements with his bow.
This castle will drink an oblation of blood
before we break its stone teeth.

That archer has seen me; he lifts his bow.
Well, the river will not bleed from his arrow.
Doubtless he would kill me if he could
and boast about it over the spilled wine;
a distant, stout, nameless man,
who would never have seen my face.

Then he would thresh about in the straw at night,
seek solace from priests, drink away memory.
But the line would have been thrown between us,
the bright gift passed, that he could not take back.
Look, he draws. If he should strike me down
I will never be so far from him again.

STEVE GRIFFITHS

There is some continuity, I hope, in my three collections. *Anglesey Material* (1980) was consciously about the place I grew up in: about returning, about the people I grew up with, and the landscapes given and made. It came with a rush of surprise: where had I been looking before? 'The Mines in sepia tint' expresses that sensation of looking everywhere but straight in the eyes of the personal history, and the poetic equivalent of that skill, which must be continuously re-learned. There's a preoccupation with justice, an awareness that it's not always so simple, something I worry at continually. There's also a dramatic sense: of confrontation, and the juxtaposition of the disparate to see what will happen.

From *Anglesey Material* I also include 'Crossing Lady Stanley, here, 1868', because it confronts, in a different political way, the smallness of social self-delusion with the elemental power of the north coast of Ynys Môn – a kind of hardnosed pathetic fallacy, because it equates the integrity in that power with the invisibility of the servant, and questions the poet's position as participant and spectator.

Three poems from *Civilised Airs* follow: 'Everyone watches the sunset' as one of a group of love-poems, with a lightness contrasting the intensity of 'Still too quick to hold', also a love poem, which celebrates being a father *through* my wife, with a sense of wonder I hope I'll never lose. The theme of parenthood began with this poem and develops into a discovery, celebration, tribute and lament, of son reaching back to discover parents, and forward as parent. The movement of time, as in 'Climber', shadows these themes.

From *Uncontrollable Fields*, I include the 'Elegy for John Tripp', who never lost that sense of ironic 'moral astonishment', while all too aware of his own imperfections. His influence is clear: Wales needed its major East European poet, and we lost him all too early. I have sacrificed the space for a greater variety of my work (particularly the London poems in *Civilised Airs*) to include 'Villa-Famès, August 1986', which celebrates, in a setting outside Wales, the deep and ancient need for the binding of community, and examines the place of ritual, and indeed violence, within that need. A lot of what I have done seems to be about belonging, and not quite belonging, at personal, family, community, and national levels, and finally, with 'The choice of flowers', in the slipperiness of time.

The Mines in sepia tint

A man beats his wife on the mountainside.

Their shouts pierce the copper drumskin
of the coming storm: the earth of copper
the heather, the copper sky:

everything rumbles round inside the drum.

the man in a grey suit, white-faced,
his eyes shifting fast and nervous
copper copper copper copper the woman
outraged by my witness of her beating

my warning shout as I passed
and my feet pounded the veins of copper
across country: then, poised on thin white legs,
doubtfully angry, wet hair plastered on my forehead,
sixteen, not knowing what to do.

They gave me silent, heated looks,
and I ran on.

Later, I wrote a poem about the pylons on the horizon.

Often I have written the wrong poem.

Crossing Lady Stanley, here, 1868

You are ensconced in your vain folly
on the cliffs. The wind would flatten
even your hair, Lady Stanley,
posed with your frilled infants.
Before dinner you imagined yourself
to be Byron, stripped of his laughter,
self-glorified in a sunset of madness:

the cries of seabirds fell on each other
as so many colours fall at the horizon,
not considering the one below
shivering and settling in the shadow
of its transformation.
Now giant winds and giant darkness
outpower the tinkling cutlery of a family feast.

Your eyes illuminate the fat candles,
a manservant attends, and a mason or two,
for you want us to know what you did with all that money:
your name is everywhere, benefactress of hospitals
and churches; purveyor of lasting graffiti,
Kilroy of the marble halls. Superseded
by Amlwch bootboys in rainy bus-shelters.

Last week, my friends probed your folly
and craned through your poor mock slits.
Lax feet turned the bean-tins in your monument,
half-curious, cameras in cases.
My face a necessary mask in a cutting wind,
I was laid flat in the heather; framed
in banks of cloud lay a lake of purest turquoise.

You stood at the edge of the colour, slight,
but there, as by the ballroom floor you might
have wanted to impress some well-lined beau.
Our minds moved together, a moment shared.
You would have shuddered at the intimacy.
You had bought this view. A carriage waited
on the mountainside, to remove it from you.

I carried our intimacy back to the van,
a fragment of eggshell,
a peasant savouring the illicit
with a little smile of gratification.
Your driver too was waiting,
with his patient, leathery face,
an impenetrable landscape.

Everyone Watches the Sunset

Everyone watches the sunset
in airport lounges waiting, groups that compose
themselves and rotate, clutching souvenirs and small change.

I carry your rough sparrowquick laugh
from the small hours,
bars of copper light from your fine hair.

In the train that carries you away
among clusters of words thrown casually
together like exiles

I could be the sound of chaffinches beyond the window,
the shadow on the carriage wall,
wearing your hat.

Still too quick to hold

The bus driver
went gently on the bends.
My son moved with the delicate swell.

A technician in dull green
scans your mound
like a vase to be dated.

All corners,
an apprehensive Gawain
at the foreseen tumulus,

I wait for the marvellous green child
to leap into view,
my instruction, my inheritance.

You lie there like someone
on the news who would like to be watching
as well as making it

and the baby's born momentarily,
a restless green sonar blur
swimming onto a screen,
refusing to pose, in absolute confidence
prodding the interior toys of mother

who will not forget, giving
bloodily under curious fingers,
one with the fish and the birds of the air:

here in the belfry hangs the heart
here the lungs, here the musical stomach
and the watery sack they bring me in,
and the lifeline to thrust aside,
swimming dangerously.

The baby leaps against the air
like a persistent salmon
rippling under the element
of my laid palms.

Beyond, over there, the haze
of time, the mountains of love,
unconcerned, apprehensive, unconcerned,
warming like damp turf an hour after dawn.

Climber

Turning at every few thigh-straining pushes
on the steep soft slope, I feel
the years raise their backs,
effort by effort

and as the unobtrusive hills rise about me,
I hear tiny breakages in the wind
that mark time, small birds
clinking like glasses over the distant stream.

Elegy for John Tripp

A man on the radio talked of soft tissue
printed on million-year riverbed
like a morning-after mattress –
and I thought of you very clear, John,

lifting a pint of dark in some dolmen basement,
regarding the sudden answers of the morning
after your stealing away, your sharp face
set in that spirit of mock astonishment
you learned to bewilder
producers of talks and tired assumptions.

I remember a belated urgency
in your face, as it turned back
watching the cultivation of soft edges,
as history, its fares paid, took off like that taxi
we tried to hail with a borrowed carafe.
There was a march full of friends' banners
and irony, probably sodden,
with a brass band and a cock-up somewhere.

On a stand in another world
the unprofitable take an unremitting review
of their leaders.
You take the salute, spilling drinks
and blood and atonement, and you break the silence
with what nearly everyone felt,
snarling at flummery, throned, waxing manic
then tender as warm buns in a paper bag
with some small forgiven fault
from your recognised gallery.

Confusion and moral astonishment,
something unfinished, an obvious instruction
unlearned: you listened and stirred tea
to the huge roaring ironies
of shopping-bag conversation
as the rust-red deep shit rose at the window.

Then you slotted the poems accurately
in the darkness between laughing teeth
in darkened smokefilled rooms
like some young boy who, they said, had
'immaculate positional play';
like the occasional sun through the steamy
windows of your café,
illuminating the brown sauce and the salt.

And you planted your ground of demands
that you never sold
for one moment of narrow-angled comfort,
brambles round tanks.
Your green armies
knitted their sharp-eyed peace,
needling hard minds,
weaving, digging, planting,
still they work and plot:
they move down out of the hills' cover
laughing their experienced laugh.

Villa-Famès, August 1986

For Fernando Almela,
and i.m. Alberto Solsona, 1947-1988

Red, soft-rock strata cut a line
of niches, shelters, age-creases
and navels in dry, strewn terraces
of erosion and collapse.
In hardened powdery space
abandoned to hawks and foxes
we were easily scattered
among fossils.
Our voices indiscreetly
defied the undersea silence
among the winds, and were lost.

In a decorated overhang
a chipped half-circle of stick-men
move with serious staves and appetite
through layers of memory and smoke.
It's their blood inundates the streets
from flood-channels high in the town.
With an arrow through him
a bull rears and falls forward
in ochre and blood,
surrounded in the grey bushes.

The afternoon gone badly awry,
firecrackers, beercans and oildrums
crash through the last of the bull's mind.

Neatfooted, barrel-chested, tossing
star on a rope with a minder, he came in
to the faces leaning forward to applaud
and the leafing back of old men
in their irony and knowing pride
for boys their children raised
who stretch and thrust and crow
their hips seasoned with wine and panic.

Their fast trainers touch
the edge of the bull's reach
to provoke the girls with fingers sucked
between their teeth:

the bull keeps coming,
he's a boxer with the odds stacked
and the crowd applaud its dreams,
his breathing
sorely intimate and provoked.

He bursts up the stairs, over a barrier
scattering runners into back yards
breaking sanctuary.
Women wave red towels for him
and he looks for his escape in lizard cracks.

He's down again, quick and light
and goaded by the curious flapping of a hat:
he fills the gap between spars
with his jarring distended trophy of a face.
He leaves a last mark in the wall of a café.

Only his tail and flanks move
and a scribble of flies
that ride his heat.
There's a questioning
unsteady stillness.

Through a field that blossoms handkerchiefs
and hands to catch his eye, he turns
to begin his last passes
to the small men running away
down his long vista.

The halter's ready.
Behind him are stick-men who poke and shout.
A beercan clatters towards him.
A father holds up his little girls to the bull.
He's wound in closer on a line
towards the butcher's laundered shorts.

The murdered bull goes up to the square,
becomes hung meat on a cross,
is elected mayor and presides
over a music shrill, lopsided, steely
with a movement of hips for his death.
There is subtle food in the clarinet and saxophone,
there are stately dark shades
on dining chairs, dressed for a nativity.
A slow colouring from the throat
of a trumpet hovers round
intimate parts that glisten in buckets
and probably reflect the stars above,
however faintly.

Six fiesta queens relax
beyond the arc lights, lounging
doe-eyed in their self-belief;
six official virgins off-duty,
marriageable somewhere between tonight
and the eighteenth century,
decorated with good hope,
strapping daughters in shawls
of intricate lace,
the village fixed on them
with a carnival tenacity
to invest in and honour their vigour
of weathered figureheads
with green shoots and a lick of paint,
their grandmothers' gold combs in their hair.

Through flaking teeth of rock
that lay broken on hillsides
run imprints of movement,
rushes of stone, stills.

A lean fox turns to watch
women once honoured
bury the thin resilience
of their voices in ploughed land.

Dry clouds crackle their long storm
like a leaf in the fist
over a parched line of almonds.

A video trained on coils of blue plumbing
in a bucket by the fountain
summoned the gut-stirring curiosities
of the Civil War:
those farmworkers who carried out
centuries of the bodies of saints and nuns
and arranged them
interestingly, in daylight
in the plenitude of their inheritance.

Scavenging in the early chill of the square
the fox looks up to the silent windows
and the sleepers behind their eyelids of stone
where blood dries quicker than music.

The choice of flowers

Through the rain's dissolute footsteps
the town's hum is a thing left on a stove,
beginning to cook on its own.
The call of a Boeing
is a fly that passes in the kitchen.
You are a warm light seen from the street,
but I am inside
and still surprised.
Something strange is happening.

I get off a bus in the wrong place
one midsummer dusk
and follow two strangers down a lane
under cascades of wild grass.
I am having an affair with fiction,
the passings, the shadow-life
of time misplaced.
The man didn't think of the woman
until it was too late.
He only thought of her when he was down,
and the thought uplifted him,
and when he saw her again he loved her,
and the years moved him.
And the woman disappeared,
there had been buttonholes and speeches
but no one there knew
that where she began was much later
when bodies had filled out
and were prone to be comic vehicles
of dignity, courage or regret
and their beauty was a thing
that contained all these.
Someone waves from a life you didn't choose,
from a line of portholes
in a temporary structure,
and you realize the corridor you walk
is a life too.
The trick of familiarity
is a perverse trick,
you are buried in the present,
longing both to rise out of it
and into it.
An illusion of daffodils in the winter gloom
is an act of will or strangeness
and its light underneath your face
makes you look like a ghost.

PAUL GROVES

I visited New York in the 1970s, and remain enthralled and appalled by the city. My first choice nods in the direction of Manhattan's sky-scrapers, Gothic organ pipes, proffered Marlboros: the whole phallic, accusatory finger-pointing of the place. Next I include 'Greta Garbo', if only because it's exact and seems popular. It won a prize some time ago.

I'd like to think my verse scores through accessibility. Betjeman, Auden, and Larkin have been exemplars. I made sure the poems that appeared in my first book – *Academe* – had all been taken by magazine editors. This was because I'm often in two minds as to what constitutes excellence, and need my hunches validated by others. Hugo Williams, for whom I have more than a passing respect, likes 'Ultima Thule' so it is included 'for your delectation'.

Poets are, we're told, a bitchy lot. This may be true. Carol Rumens, writing memorably in *Poetry Review*, claims 'they mostly hate each other's guts'. 'The Awful Caverns' addresses the situation.

The motor car, though obviously convenient, has a lot to answer for in terms of disrupting rural calm. I was brought up in east Mon-mouthshire where little challenged the birdsong, and television was a thing of the future. Britain has lost a good deal of innocence since the 1940s, and so have I. 'Children Playing' is included because it harks back to the golden age of my childhood, and if that's a resound-ing cliché too bad. 'The Girls at St Catherine's' appears for a similar reason.

There's much to be said for simplicity and naivety. St Matthew 18:3 sums it up nicely: 'Except ye...become as little children, ye shall not enter into the kingdom of heaven.' 'Making Love to Marilyn Monroe' constitutes a sizeable contrast. If a second quote may be permitted, one is reminded of Malcolm Muggeridge's solemn pronouncement: 'The orgasm has replaced the Cross as the focus of longing and the image of fulfilment.'

The last three inclusions are (a) about adolescent playfulness abut-ting adult guilt; (b) *vers de société* with a difference; and (c) a complemen-tary piece wherein Shelley's claim (echoing that of Dr Johnson) is gently scrutinized.

Most of the ten poems rhyme. This is because I prefer order to its alternative. It's what comes of being conservative or, if you're into psychoanalysis, anal-retentive.

A Look Around New York

Grand Guignol. It is not enough to buy
Flowers on Sixth Avenue, or books
In Greenwich Village; nor is it enough
To see *Potemkin* for the zillionth time,
Odessa steps or not. No, what we love

Is something else. Forget the classy looks
Of Bloomingdale's and Macy's. Come, let's fly.
Welcome to the sanctuaries of crime.

He takes me to the barber shop where, in
Nineteen fifty seven, Anastasia
Met his end. 'The bullets really flew!'
Gallo, his assassin, was rubbed out
Himself in April, nineteen seventy two.
Umberto's Clam House. 'Don't let all this faze yuh
– They merely reaped the harvest of the sin
They earlier sowed. Enjoyable?' No doubt;

I am the guest, and must not be ungracious.
'Now here's one for the limey. 72nd
Street. December, nineteen eighty. Does
That ring a bell?' His Buick has the answer.
It always had. A teenager, he'd buzz
The town for hours each night – or so he reckoned.
I gravely nod. The formidable, spacious
Dakota block. I hope he dies of cancer

Or cardiac arrest, and not through being
Gunned down in the foyer of the Plaza
(Hardenbergh, its architect, designed
Lennon's landmark), or one day some brash
Murder freak might similarly find
Delight in such a guided tour. It has a
Grim appeal admittedly – like seeing
Stray dogs urinate, or windblown trash.

His duty done, we home to his apartment,
A bijou residence in Union City,
Old-ladyish, no hint of vile disaster.
We tackle sushi followed by a yokan
And green-tea ice cream, then we play canasta.
He lets me win. We smoke a little shit. He
Is human, too, and probably at heart meant
To honour me with his best social token.

Greta Garbo

A Japanese paparazzo photographer has been waiting outside
her apartment for more than three years but has never suc-
ceeded in getting a full-face picture

Mostly you get the din of the Franklin D. Roosevelt Drive,
traffic plying this throughway beside
the East River. Mostly you get the sense
of being alive, of being five time zones from home,
from that family rooftree in Kawasaki, one block
from the Sojiji Temple. I have captured
kids playing patball at one two-fiftieth of a second
at f4, leaves drifting to the ground on East 52nd
at proportions of that speed, but
Dame Fortune stays elusive. For thirty-eight months
she has not bought zucchini. I find this remarkable.
The Americans call a swede a rutabaga;
I call this Swede the whole vocabulary,
depending on my mood: witch, goddess, foil, mantrap.
It is as if she never lived, and all I have done
for a slice of my life is kick cans,
light up another Lucky Strike, hope yet again
to strike lucky. I suppose this is an odyssey
in pursuit of elusiveness itself, a quest
for the resurrection of beauty: Odysseus
blew a decade on his errand. There's time yet.
When the wind blows, desperate, down from Maine,
and it's thirty below, I curse and stamp
and spend all day in the diner, wiping
condensation from the pane, focusing.
He brings me soup, and tuts, scratching his head.
'I thought Polacks were the limit, but
you're something else.' Life has become
a philosophical acceptance of loss, a conflation
of zilch and Zen. Something stirs,
but it is only the janitor humping garbage
onto the sidewalk for the next collection.
She made a movie called *Joyless Street*
in 1925, the year my mother was born
high in the hills near Kawakami
where the snowflakes are huge, and the air silent.

Ultima Thule

An initial result of Eskimo contact with whites was the Floradora Sextet,
an amateur can-can line of native girls

Number One is not used to the smoke. Eyes get
bejewelled with tears. She keeps smiling.
Number Two is fascinated by the intestines
of the trombone. It glints like narwhal tusks.
Number Three is, as usual, taciturn. She dances,
according to the Yank impresario, like an elephant.
This leaves her nonplussed. What is an elephant?
Number Four is the baby of the party. At thirteen
she is even less able to differentiate art from tomfoolery.
Number Five is Number Two's sister. She, at seventeen,
is having her first period. She feels like whalemeat.
Number Six has devised their routine. It entails
showing strange southerners underclothes in the name
of Terpsichore. The introduction of camiknickers
is a Greek gift. No such garment suits the ampleness
for which local women are renowned. High cheekbones.
Twelve left feet. An aurora borealis of petticoats.
The hall fills up: men desperate for release
from cold celibacy, enforced exposure to a lack
of Boston or Sacramento. The ivories are vamped,
a flenching of doubt, as certainty strides centre stage.
'Gentlemen...' He speaks with force but without conviction.
'The Cream of the Arctic, the Passion Flowers
of Prudhoe Land – I give you, for your delectation...'
Number Three has to be dragged forward into the wings.
Her inflamed face aches in the mirror. 'Floradora,'
she says, her mouth full of stones. 'What do we *mean*?'

The Awful Caverns

*I didn't realise how deeply
some poets hate and distrust other poets*
        Gavin Ewart, *Laser*

I'd thought they would be extra nice
    and shine like any star did:
'Do come and see me. Don't think twice...'
    Instead I find them guarded.

I'd thought most would extend a hand:
    'We're all in this together,
sharing an exciting land
    of words and wisdom.' Never.

I fondly had assumed my peers,
    my fellow seers and sages,
would walk unfettered down the years
    across the shining pages,

noble as gods, their glowing pens
    poised to set life singing.
I should have had a shade more sense.
    Perhaps it's my upbringing –

looking for the best in folk,
    trusting human nature
to rise above the knowing joke,
    the snide, uncaring feature.

Churlishness is commonplace.
    Acid wits are honed.
Darkness broods on many a face.
    'I'm so glad that you phoned.

Yes, let's meet up. I love your verse.
    And – what's that – you like mine?'
It's rarely heard. Instead, some curse
    sends tingles down a spine.

Suspicion, venom, jealousy
   lurk beneath veneers
as thin as paper. Acrid glee
   permeates the years

like rain through limestone scenery,
   eroding, slow and sly....
Beneath the surface greenery
   the awful caverns lie.

Children Playing

They do not know it, but they are
dancing towards the edge of dance,
like a drunk cartoon mouse on a table.
Adulthood is waiting to swallow play,
digest it and defecate it to enrich the soil
of its own cramped gardens, with prams,
nappies, a sleeping greenhouse dreaming of stones.

They are reproducing the enemies of childhood:
mummies and daddies, the one ironing on a bank
of green, tidying cowslip cuffs, dandelion collars,
the other relaxing in an armchair of bracken,
sucking a pipe of grass, reading *The Air News*
easily in arms which will never tire of the pages.
The land reaches out to them, offers the sweets

of innocency, and the clouds are congenial gestures.
The brooks run clear with a told-you-so, told-you-so
babble over trinket stones. How strangely
the grey pastures of commitment and responsibility
allure; how much more driving to work magnetizes
as myth than rolling over and over down
this rich hillside for ever.

The Girls at St Catherine's

What is it about the girls at St Catherine's:
Saintliness? No. Innocence? Ignorance means

The same thing at that age. To know is to be guilty of
Adulthood of a sort, to fall in love

Simply a commitment to the unprecedented
Experience. By soap scented

Rather than by perfume, by exercise rouged rather
Than by cosmetics, they stroll under a lather

Of cherry blossom. It is April in their lives.
Manhood hangs somewhere like a rack of knives.

Making Love to Marilyn Monroe

He pumps her up, po-faced, his right leg rising
And falling wearisomely. Breasts inflate,
Thighs fatten, force and perseverance raising
A rubber spectre. Plump, comical feet
Swell into being, but her eyes stay dead.
Her crotch arrives: exaggerated, furry.

Five minutes and she's full. Pink. Somewhat odd.
His brother brought her over on the ferry
From Hook of Holland, folded flat beneath
Shirts and trousers. Bought in Amsterdam,
She needed only an awakening breath,
Divine afflatus nurturing the dream

Till it becomes substantial. When she's tight
He plugs her with a stopper, tests for leaks
With an embrace, marvels at each huge teat,
And stands back slightly to admire her looks.
She leans against the sofa at an angle,
Legs amply parted, lips a sullen pout.

Like Mae West she might mutter 'I'm no angel'
If able to articulate. Her pert
Expression is the only clue he'll get
To how she feels. If he but had a wand
He'd *ping* her into life, but all she's got
To offer him is quick relief and wind.

He gets it over with, lights turned down low.
Pneumatic gasps were absent. Self-esteem
Plummets, yet she was an easy lay.
He puts her in the wardrobe till next time.
The sorry fact is real women don't
Fancy him. A shrink would understand.

Who are so inflated that no dent
Disfigures them? Some men need to get stoned
Before they do it; some touch little girls....
At least this shady rigmarole can bring
Release without distress. Contentment gels.
Doubt punctures with a quintessential bang.

Something Nasty in the Woodshed

'The bulb is a prostate gland',
Peterson said, adjusting
His metalwork goggles, 'and
If you heat it the mercury rises.'
His eyes were bright; he was lusting
After taboo surprises,

Contraband thrills. The burner
Was lit, the thermometer held
Above it. I was a slow learner;
But Peterson was thrilled.
'Sex is like this,' he asserted;
'It's a physical change.' I blurted

Out something about the danger
Of what he was doing, but
He assured mé he was no stranger
To science, to test tube and prism,
To his father's garden hut.
'Soon you will have an orgasm

As the pressure builds up, and the top
Blows with a moment of joy.'
I repeated that we ought to stop
The experiment, but he was wetting
His lips, the incredible boy,
Like Newton and Faraday, petting,

His hand up history's skirt.
'What if something goes wrong?'
'One of us will get hurt –
At least,' he grinned. A bang.
Glass splintered. The dangerous game
Climaxed. Mercury came.

not starting from the top.
I hope you did not mind me
    rising to a stop.
So this is how you find me –

    feet, decanting woes.
that creep about on wary
    and mean as much as those
Words can be light and airy

    or sweep it from the room.
and symbol-ridden parlance,
    the poet's sense of doom
now and then can balance

    a little levity
unrelievedly serious;
    when poetry must be
I feel it's deleterious

    and hardly something worse.
eliciting a snigger
    out of a page of verse,
an unfamiliar figure

    a small attempt to cut
essentially it's harmless,
    and artificial, but
The project may seem charmless

    On this what is your view?
a poem written backwards.
    rather than bend them to
One might be wise to lack words

    while passing on his bike.
a vicar pulling faces
    perverse, perhaps, and like
Starting from the base is

Turvy-Topsy

Unacknowledged Legislator

The poet has a poem accepted.
He tells his wife he is happy.
The cow jumped over the moon.
They are building motorway.
He gets twelve pounds.
Concorde refuels.

The poet has a poem rejected.
He tells his wife he is no longer happy.
Someone else gets twelve pounds.
The motorway inches forward.
Concorde farts thousands
in hot air.

The poet has another poem accepted.
He believes this makes two.
Twenty-four pounds accumulates.
It is June already.
Thirteen American movies
have been started since January,

each with a budget beyond his wildest stanzas.
He updates daffodils.
Wordsworth did not have a patent on clouds
he thinks bravely.
He submits a poem hymning cumulonimbus.
It is promptly rejected.

Why? he asks. Why?
Do not the editor and I speak the same language?
Are we not kindred spirits?
Did we not both take degrees
in English Literature?
It is August, and someone he has not met

tops the charts and starts a European tour.
Five thousand pounds a week
and all she had
was a CSE in domestic science.
Somebody in the City makes a killing.
The poet treads on a snail

on his way to the postbox.
Is this inauspicious? he wonders.
He deposits the envelope hesitantly.
He walks back avoiding the cracks
in the paving stones.
He daydreams about thirty-six pounds.

DOUGLAS HOUSTON

'The Others', the earliest poem here, represented an advance by adopting a quasi-fictive mode. It was also among the first of my poems to enjoy the enthusiastic approval of mentors and fellow-poets in Hull, where about half my first collection was written, including the following two.

'Devotions' is a more thorough-going projection of experience into the modality of fiction, which was accompanied by a step beyond repeated versions of the pentameter with its incantational twelve-syllable line.

'Sic Transit' is one of several brief pieces in *With the Offal Eaters* to attract favourable comment. I include it partly as a corrective to my inferiority complex or ambitiousness, wanting poems to go at least thirty lines to be worth having written.

The remaining poems were written in Wales. 'Lines on a Van's Dereliction' is significant to me for having begun in idle technical dabblings and turning itself into a poem, an encouraging phenomenon in times of drought. Its imagery indicates a change of environment, as does 'On the Beach', memorable for a gratifying spontaneity of composition: it took about thirty minutes, and needed little subsequent tuning. 'On the Beach' has been of value to others in similar predicaments, and I like it for convincing me that 'the profane and unprofitable art' can be more than a vain satisfaction.

Of the remaining poems, each in a coming collection, 'Tramontane' is the earliest, an attempt at politicized poetry partly prompted by Sean O'Brien's achievement in *The Frighteners*. It ends up as an 'Aberystwyth fantasia', but in doing so makes use of elements which had been sketched out in Germany ten years before.

'Pictograph' is a love poem, though, as far as spontaneity goes, at certain points it was blood from a stone. I don't write many love poems, so I include it from a sort of gratitude that it insisted on getting written.

'Taliesin: Interim Report' conjures *y Bardd* as the Spirit of Poetry undergoing historical dispossession and cynically surfacing in Thatcher-land. It's another I was pleased with for any success it has as a fictionalized exposition of a set of cultural and personal circumstances.

'Consultative Document' is more solidly earthed in contemporary actuality, but is nonetheless liberally salted with imaginative elements. This is one of the latest things I've written, and I hope it's a vein I can work more fully.

The Others

I am not the man who sits alone
At a rustic table in a pub garden,
But as he turns his head to watch me pass
I admire his solitary love of air.

The man who always knows when leap-years are,
Whose papers are all in immaculate order,
Is more of a stranger – aloof, I suspect,
So I call him *The Pocket Book of Boredom*.

Others constitute a powerful faction;
Their numbers are not to be taken lightly
In assessing the management of a life.
Study one or two, but keep your distance.

Their variety is overwhelming.
How they united I don't know,
But the undertaker's assistant,
Tactful as rollers under a coffin,

Delicate girls who work in flower-shops,
Every Chinese person in the world,
All those who wear uniforms or nothing,
Are beyond my first person singular.

Despite occasional hostilities
By and large they have been good to me.
Lately I agree with them on many points,
Though I hear of their internal differences.

It is my hope that these will be resolved.
I'd be foolish to take this for granted,
Each of them finally in my position,
Having seen nasty behaviour, some of it mine.

Devotions

Having mortified myself with a hangover,
Deliberately conceived on two days' hard drinking,
I am standing underneath the end of the pier
In the year's high ritual of my seagull worship,
Which demands such unbreakfasted, humbling rigours,
And will culminate with prostration in the surf
After the solemn dispensation of breadcrusts.

A friend, long of the behaviourist persuasion,
Calls worship a proper respect got out of hand,
The mystery of the gulls beyond his dissections
To trace why what is done is done just as it is –
A closed-circuit, tape-loop mentality to me,
Only to be envied the comfort of closed doors
And confidence in the given human reasons.

He laughs at the Botanical Salvationists
Whose resurrection is the pot-plant of one's choice,
But I'd become a *nephrolepis exaltata*
Sooner than a name unsought in some register,
And their watering rites have great delicacy.
I have given him a pectoral of feathers,
And wait for him to bow, like the dove, to the gull.

I have time for Devotees of Telegraph Poles.
Sighting along their black totems at certain stars,
They believe light is soluble in midnight rain,
That high winds snatch beams from outlying farmhouses
And anglers' lamps, then mix the stuff into wet air,
Which the poles absorb to transmit the stars their light.
A simple religion, but lacking daylight truth.

I have risen now, soaked and icily refreshed,
From the white fringes of the sea where I have lain
The required fifteen minutes. Their cries above me
Worked sacred hypnosis, each mew a blade of truth.
Some of the sand from my clothes and skin will be kept
To be rubbed in my beard every Monday, run through
My fingers daily until next year's renewal.

Sic Transit

The glory of the world is passing already
With white blossoms dropping from the may's laden boughs.
The heels of the man with shattered kneecaps crush them
To a moist translucency. Dead prisoners gather
On the green outside the Methodist Hall to hear
A moving address on human rights delivered

By a visiting Belgian milkman, who breaks down
When whispers inform him of a lost football match.
People who happened to be listening to radios
Maintained their politic silence while descending
To shelters now crowded and firmly closed.

Lines on a Van's Dereliction

'Farewell! thou art too dear for my possessing.'

This rust-infested cage with worn-out brakes,
Green paintwork scratched as if a demon clawed it,
Calls forth these tribute lines for old times' sake –
It's future's scrap, I simply can't afford it.
The engine's blown some seal that keeps the oil in,
The windows seem the only parts intact;
Though recently I screwed a brand-new coil in,
Such costly items will no more exact
The cash from me to keep it on the road.
Permit me now the vocative, O van,
Defeated by that last excessive load,
The tons of logs your brakes tried to withstand
In huge momentum down the mountainside;
For many thousand miles I've driven you,
A third-hand emblem of a sort of pride,
But now the year is 1982,
Your time, at thirteen years, is up I think.
In olive groves or by the sea we parked you,
Our four-wheeled bedroom-wine-bar-kitchen-sink;
On that first trip the Florence police remarked you
And towed you off for us to go your bail,
But recollection's pasta can't obscure
The fact that now your braking power's failed
We'd like a vehicle just a wee bit *newer*.
So farewell now old heap, have fun as tins.
One day within the geochronic system
Digesting contents of all rubbish bins
My big toe might encounter your third piston.
We'll render gaseous traces to the sky
While mineral satisfactions of the earth

Redistribute our atoms by and by.
Infinity's before us right from birth;
So don't take it too badly, rusty friend,
Should I dismember you to sell as parts;
Remember being doesn't simply end,
Disintegration's where the big time starts.

On the Beach

Recall the near-drowning of your son
Through the deception of a pool's shelved floor,
And think your thanks beneath this clear blue sky
You were allowed the diving dash to save him.
Be grateful also, while the mountains' vast indifference
Inland and the miles of sea and sand force
A glad acceptance of powerless unimportance,
That the woman walking with you is beautiful
In this sun, and lovelier by the small light
Beside her bed, although she is not that son's mother,
And that he and his brother, whose presences
You imagine playing here, are always absent now,
And living, somewhere, where you cannot see them;
Dreams in which filial love inundates you,
The loss you feel when watching small boys' games,
Come like a rain to rust the bright metal of days
To uselessness, and what you call your heart
Can't tell what it wills, this present love or a time
When these sons may be wholly yours once more,
Who will always be yours either side of the grave.
But admit it is worth what the righteous call rejoicing
To be linked in a threesome with a woman who loves you
By her little daughter's hands. Without pretending
This child is yours, her happiness when mother's and your arms
Lift her to bear her through the air on your walk
Crosses the opened borders of your feelings
Like provisions a beleaguered people crave.
Believe your eyes that this is the world,
That the huge assuagement of the beach and the sea,
Their mild colours and unstrained continuity,
Can allegorize your life as satisfactorily

As the derelict structures in pathless forests
Posited for the poems that, thank God, you do not write.
In this air you barely remember the invidious need
For cigarettes where breathing itself is stimulating.
Examine what the child gives you, the razor fish
Smaller than any you've seen, almost too fragile
To touch with these fingers of yours, so its brittle arc
Instructs you in gentleness. Take it home,
With the iridescent chip of shell, the traces of sand
That will lodge a long time in the seams of your pockets,
And, now you have written these hours' memorial
In verse as easy as the walk you took,
Go back sometime to Ynyslas, with Karen and Little El.

Tramontane

'It is a play no rationalist would write' – John Tripp

Within the glassed box of the bus-shelter
A youth whose head is bowed, whose lower lip droops,
With difficulty or absorption, over what he reads
Stares at an introductory page signed
In facsimile by its one-book author,
Whose spikily legible hand reveals
Mein Kampf (in English) still commands attention.
Its regrettably credible thesis,
Syllogistically pairing man and beast,
Persists in consequences of its consequences
Beside the harbour. While mast-pulleys rattle
In November wind that makes the rigging wires sing,
The proprietor of the town's best restaurant
Becomes once more what he'd rather not be,
A displaced German drunk whose lopsided smile
Attempts the maintenance of appearances
While, awash with self-pity and *Gewürztraminer*,
He explains himself to the fixtures and fittings,
Emotively reiterating *Stalingrad, Stalingrad*
Sechste Armee, mein Vater ist in Stalingrad gefallen...
His chef has heard it all before, supposes
He'll pull himself together by this evening

When members of a political committee
Will dine there with their party's *Wunderkind*,
The Right Honourable Member for Ponsley Mongford,
Whose 'forward in strength' speech has boosted morale
Throughout the nation, brought him to such places as this.
The absence of a stalwart of long standing,
The Chairman of the local British Legion,
Whose lungs that filled with oil in '41
Gave up while he was out of town on holiday,
Will tone the jollity down while he's remembered;
His coffin is detraining as the *Journal*,
Which takes municipal pride in his obituary,
Is dumped in bundles at the station news-stand.
Only dispersing vapour trails detract
From the sky's blue perfection of emptiness
Above ornate frontages of old brick
That rich light reddens to their nature as baked earth
While smooth wheels bear the body on its penultimate stage
Towards a small cemetery on a steep incline
Where spirit-level and plumb-bob contrive
A regimented neatness that's impressive from a distance.
The barber opposite the taxi-rank
Glimpses the hearse departing in his mirror,
Knows who it is, recalls the old boy's trims
And their agreement in baffled disaffection
With the interest rates and crude utilitarianism
Of the government they'd both helped to elect.
He's casting a more neutral vote next time,
He informs his customer's reflection
In the immediate foreground of the glass.
The conversation moves on to guest-houses,
Unhurried scissors ceasing for point-making pauses
During which his eyes fix those in the mirror
With practised earnestness that's disconcerting
In one whose skills are paid for to cut hair.

The light fades and the tide is coming in
When the man who hopes to be next summer's sensation
As 'Wales's Greatest Sand-Sculptor' abandons
The Last Supper (his ninth, improved, attempt)
To dissolution and a distinctly vinous German
Who, having tried to buy it, pressed ten pounds in his hand
Because it was *wunderschön, wunderschön.*

Far out at sea the horizon's distorting lens
Gently squeezes the blood-orange sun out of sight
As the surf begins carving sharp concavities
In the tableau's base. The restaurateur cries a little,
Then continues the walking, the breathing of ozone,
That will leave him feeling more or less sober,
And *shrecklich*, but ready, he thinks, for the booking
With their guest and their money from beyond the mountains.

Pictograph

'if I enlarge, I see nothing but the grain...and if I do not enlarge, if I content myself with scrutinizing, I obtain this sole knowledge, long since possessed at first glance: that this indeed has been' – Roland Barthes, *Camera Lucida*

You, in your youth, that has hardly ended,
Wearing only a river from the hips down,
Advance past glassy shallows to a fast pool
Shadowed by abundance of overhanging trees,
Where braided roots and sinewy vegetation
Give the far bank a satyr's musculature.
Over your shoulder you smile at the camera,
Inviting to immersion's cool delight,
Calling me in from nine years' distance,
Where it's December and what you excite
Requires a new tense called the *sexual present*
Expressing how in both kind and degree
My youth and forty years feel this alike.
The confident foliage, the unblemished light
On your nakedness all acknowledge summer;
By means of powerful lenses, I descend
Through sycamore leaves to grainy generalizations,
And might as well be a bird in this photograph,
Held in my course through its myth of your pleasure,
As here, glimpsing these thin clouds I exhale
But feeling no more cold than you seem to,
My knowing *ingénue*, clasped intimately
By clarities of water, light, and air.
Slipped through the aperture's instant you become
Discontinuous with your past and future,

Your reflection stilled in its fluid shimmer,
A white encrustation of turbulence fixed
Almost modestly where your full curves submerge.

Weeks pass through which I frequently consider
This photograph that came with marrying you,
Extrapolating only a thin frame
Of parallels linking *now* and preterite *thens*:
How once, nine miles upstream and years before,
I too bathed in this river where its thrust
Slows at a deep cleft in lead-bearing rock;
How recently we followed its lowland ogees
Going to renew your friendship with the girl
Whose father's eye behind the viewfinder
Composed my sanctuary against the winter
Where luminous significances congregate.
Transmitting news that thought and flesh accord
Through easy registers of sensation,
Your smile subverts totalitarian cold,
Alleviates the stringencies that police
Belief cordoned inside severity's ghetto.
The depths of shade and light in all its manners,
From sequin-flicks to elemental white,
Provide your setting and an image of you,
Whose face's lovely chiaroscuro drew me
Here to pause, and sense the dawning certainty
That you are all I sought within your picture.

Taliesin: Interim Report

'I am Taliesin. I sing perfect metre,
Which will last to the end of the world.'
        – for Jaroslaw Kosciuszko

No big men now whose mountainside camp-fires
Glimpsed from the bay hushed sea-going mendicants,
Who for my verses fat with flattery
Saw me all right for wine and bagged gold,
From whose superfluities of women and horses
I made my selections and left.

Power dripped from those wilds slowly, squeezed
By the long closure of armies, dogma;
Then centuries, successively more chancy –
Getting killed in a pub in Deptford that time,
Called mad or treacherous, a saint or drunkard,
Increasingly prone to such miscalculations
As my verbal elixirs lost efficacy
To charm my ample perquisites from fortunes
Glittering their transits down the generations.

Like a well outside an expired village
I shed my usefulness, stared blankly skyward,
And, bound to language, was spouse to silence
When money assumed a god's taciturnity.
I survived Victoria as an ivied headstone
Incised with twenty of Milton's syllables:
But O the heavy change, now thou art gone,
Now thou art gone, and never must return.
The wars got ridiculous: 500 pounds
Of high explosive by air from Krefeld
Blew me back into the routine of birth.

It took me twenty years to find the chieftains,
Bored at the ends of their heavy oak tables,
Amusing themselves with numerical riddles
They try to solve by juggling variables
Of unit costs and fealty of workers.
I sing their processes, breathe life into their products,
I glorify them in the halls of their reports;
Their gratitude for perfect punctuation
And sweet modalities framing persuasions,
For my priesthood of the unsplit infinitive,
Is shown in the miniature poems they make
Of my name and some figures on slips of stiff paper,
Admitting me to deference, worlds of choice.

Consultative Document

I

High above streets infested with ordinariness
And wired to equivalent levels of interest,
A sealed chamber houses work and sleep.
His absence is rank with sweating air-fresheners
Stifling the half-life of 60-a-day.
A moral code guessed at in fresh vegetables
Is rotting in the refrigerator.
He is heading out in his big white dirigible,
Aimed as always down motorways
At the *terra incognita* of the first million.

Shaman of the commercial jungle,
He confronts the Spirit of Investment
On behalf of diffident factory owners,
Causing funding in cloudbursts sufficient
To germinate employment, buy new equipment,
Pay his percentage. While he sleeps
In his fashion in the scheduled city
Nightshifts clank out what he has wrought;
Automated electroplating plants
Start heating their acid and cyanide solutions
That time is not lost when men clock on at eight.
When his body is passing through the machinery
Of a risky deal, pain like grey metal-vapour
Infects his lieutenants,
Is beyond the endurance of secretaries.

II

But it feels good this morning,
Confident, easy, driving west
On expensive engineering, out past the churned mud
Of sites memorializing abandoned motives,
Till a January dawn flashes from puddles
Down long perspectives of level fields.
Arrived, there's the usual tour of the works,
The fuming vats, the precision components
For launching missiles, steering torpedoes,

Displayed at the tips of executive fingers;
Blue flame-plasma roars its mach-1 shroud
Blasting nickel onto drums for radioactive waste.
I make detailed notes; this report will be interesting.
His cheque's square inches will cover distaste,
Buy out ingratitude's assent to objections.

MIKE JENKINS

Choosing poems for this anthology was both pleasurable and difficult. If I'd acted impulsively, there's little doubt I'd have chosen the last ten or so I'd written: believing the latest to be the best.

As it is, I've gone for variety of style and subject-matter, but still missed out certain areas such as my dialect poems, more overtly satirical ones and the long poems (which don't lend themselves to extraction). However, an unexpected bonus was the opportunity I took to revise earlier poems, though not radically.

This selection moves outwards from the self (with 'I') to my family with such as 'Creature', to individuals important to me in 'Survivor', into history with 'Dic Dywyll' and, finally, dealing with death in '"He loved light, freedom and animals"'.

In the past, I've been called a local (Merthyr) poet, an urban poet and a political poet and I hope this selection will both prove and confound those terms. Living on the edge of a moor still owned by the Coal Board, teaching at a school overlooking the Brecon Beacons yet drawing pupils from council estates and older communities and, above all, seeing politics in terms of people's lives: all these contribute to a tension which questions categories.

Although not an obvious presence, the Welsh language is a significant underlying influence on my poetry. I hear it in work, I learn it and my children go to a Welsh-medium school: it's a measure of our striving for identity, as well as a pervasive sound. But to reject English as the language of colonization, would be to dismiss its shaping of my past and its vitality in the lives of most of my nation; a vitality which poetry should enrich.

I

I is the biggest word
in the English language:
some people yawn bored
as soon as you mention it.

I know people who erect crosses
made from it
and then refuse to carry them.

I know people who build extensions
onto it and call
those extensions their children.

I know people who would
like to keep changing it
every week with fashionable clothing.

I know people who hate it so much
it's become an obsession,
like a priest always ranting against sin.

In English, 'I' begins the sentence:
the other words queue up behind it
waiting for their instructions.

You must write 'I' with a capital letter
but 'we' with a small one.
Why?.... Well...as in God and Great Britain.

i know a person who tries to make it
mock itself, to disguise ambition.
i know a person who thinks it will outlive
the exploring body, the inflated mind.

Creature

Last night the sea heaved up a creature,
one I could not explain.

Half-boat, half-animal it seemed:
ribs of rusted tin, skull smooth as plastic.

My daughter played in its house of bones,
bouncing pebbles like syllables ringing.

She kept asking its name, how old was it?
Was it a dragon? Oil like blood dripped.

'I don't know!' I said (sounding unscientific);
she pulled out bolts of its neck to sit on.

I pursued it in books: the Bible dumb.
She ran in and out of its tunnel of questions.

The Beach, my Son and the alltime Batman

We drape ourselves down
we are the same
as those posing we condemn
soaking up sunlight
not innocently but complacently
reading about it
as chemicals magnify the rays
we drive along we buy
the things that cannot burn.

My son has made his nest
in front of me I tell him
of the north and ice melting
the next flood the cities
are a ball the oceans
a bat above them
the hole above us widens
we will fall upwards
into the gap and together
drift into space.

The cities drown as the tide
hurries in and people quickly
busy their belongings he sees
the need to swim
but how can we learn
to swim in space?
there is no air the tanks
will surely drag us down.

That night he dreams catastrophe
the trees have lost their skin
they all drop to the ground
and roots break up
into pieces of a desert
but God the alltime Batman
comes to the rescue when
my son lifted to a cloud
rides to the sun
makes peace between
Water and Fire at last
so everything grows a beginning.

Canine Graffiti

Some loopy boy wrote 'FUCK OFF'
in firm felt-tip on the white back
of a nippy-as-a-ferret Jack Russell.

Senior Staff spotted it while it shat
in the midst of a modern dance
formation – leotards snapped!

(When they weren't busy piercing ears
with sharp instructions, or spiking hair
with swift backhand cuffs,

they did have time to snoop on lessons
which exceeded the statutory decibel rate.)
They set off in pursuit of the errant dog,

skilfully hurdling its poop in the process.
They chased it into Mathematics
where it caused havoc by lifting a leg

45° towards the blackboard's right-angle.
Then through the Audio-Visual concepts room,
across the film of Henry V, making Olivier's horse

rear and throw the bewildered actor.
It hid behind a smoke-screen in the bogs,
sniffed out bunkers in the coal-bunker.

For hours it disappeared and Senior Staff
suspected a trendy English teacher
of using it as an aid to creative writing.

Finally, it was duly discovered
by Lizzie Locust (Biology), necking
with a stuffed stoat in the store-cupboard.

Now you can see the distraught Headmistress
scrubbing from bell to bell in her office,
a small dog held down by burly, sweating prefects.

Survivor

They came from the arterial streets
of Dowlais, to the pill-box estate
wired to the hillside. Married
too young, for their bodies' sake.

You were, at first, a novelty
won at a fair. Then you cried
every night, dragging them from calm
of a deep sleep like a premature
birth again and again.......
until he learnt to slumber and snore
nailed by bottles to his marriage-bed.
You grew up doing the opposite
of all the examples they set.

Now you smile survival at me,
like one of those old Dowlais buildings:
the Library propped by scaffolding
(friends hold you steady).
If I searched long enough
in the archives of your mind
perhaps I'd find a reason.

The time your father's bayonet-case
came down like a truncheon
onto your mam, you couldn't hide
behind their smoke or fan the fire
any longer. You hit his helmet-head,
so he struck out and you lay
like an imitation of the dead.

Tracey – the common name belies you.
You have reclaimed the black hills
of night with your boys on stolen bikes.
The sound of their engines
worries round and round your mother
as she sits and knits alone.
Your father's in a cot
crazily shaking its bars.

A Newt in the Classroom

At first, I took it
for a plastic practical joke.

But she picked him up
and he walked, out of his aqua-sphere,
like a man on the moon.

I grasped the moment, as she had
the lizard. Holding the idea by its tail.
We dissected him with words.
We passed him along rows
like a thought too icy to hold.

He was a clay god
each made in their own image.
The sensitive Australian girl
railing against his imprisonment
in the grey box of her classroom.
The boy who tried to get inside
the skin so much he shrank
into a different dimension.
Too many calling him 'cute':
mistrusting their senses, even
their over-exhausted sight.

Under the sun of our attention
he was rapidly drying up:
'Get water from the Lab!'
'No, she'll cut him up!'

By Friday, he had died.
Turned white as blank paper,
while our walls were filled
with creations glued on
like his tail sticking to your palm.

An Escape

On the mantelpiece, my mother's trophies
stand in line and wink at me.
They collect any sunlight
in our shabby room, where carpet stains
are bruises...his jealousy
those dents she couldn't dust away.

My Mam's at work again, on the tills
handling all that money which flows
through her like the facts
they funnel into me at school.
Keeping the doors on their hinges,
keeping the bailiffs from biting
harder than any Big Freeze.

I wipe the condensation with my sleeve:
its smear like snot. I peer
through a film of dirt and damp
at dog-packs worrying the bins.
They search and tear for scraps,
their hunger sharpening canines.
Find more than in our kitchen!

It's the rain I despise...nagging me inside
with memories of screaming, fighting:
'Oh no! Dad!'...'Get away, you bastard son!'

But here comes Lisa with our dog
and her friends all wild in the wind;
and we're off to the little river,
to the tree-trunk bridge where our heads
will be leaf-light and reeling.

Reflection in a Reservoir

It was a time of light
a camera would have to be patient
as an angler to catch:
the church spires of conifers
and brick-colour of larch
suddenly drowned in the valley.

Somehow, in the reflection I expected
to see the spires brought to earth
and changed to sturdy chapels
(once barns storing Welsh)
and the larches to be stretched
into a cart-clogged village street.

But the water was soon struck hard
into a dark-grey metal they'd melt
and dam in offices, ready to weigh
its worth. Would it become
the colour of coal by night-time?

Dic Dywyll

Dic Dywyll (Dick Dark) was a renowned balladeer in 19th-
century Merthyr. He was blinded working at Crawshay's
ironworks. His daughter, Myfanwy, was immortalized
in Joseph Parry's song.

I have banished God
further than the Antipodes
since my so-called accident.
He was the owner
of those mills of death,
his manager the old Cholera.
The preaching of Cheapjack remedies:
holding up heaven as a cure.

They took my eyes
and struck them
into cannon-balls.
My mask and its perpetual night
is known to the pit-ponies.

Crossing the Iron Bridge
I hear the river's voice
bring tune to my ballads
and hooves of canal-horses
count beats, pauses come
as I breathe the welcome wind
from the west and eventual sea.

Night arrives and they all
share my mask: punchy drunkards,
rousing rebels and laughing ones
who sup to conquer daytime.

My daughter is the blackbird
bringing fire to the hearth
of our basement with her song;
while I'm the owl, turning
to face their sufferings,
calling out to chase away
the chimneys' shadows. Masters
I magic to mice
under the death's-head moon.

'He loved light, freedom and animals'

An inscription on the grave of one of the children who
died in the Aberfan disaster of 21 October 1966.

No grave could contain him.
He will always be young
in the classroom
waving an answer
like a greeting.

Buried alive –
alive he is
by the river
skimming stones down
the path of the sun.

When the tumour on the hillside
burst and the black blood
of coal drowned him,
he ran forever
with his sheepdog leaping
for sticks, tumbling together
in windblown abandon.

I gulp back tears
because of a notion of manliness.
After the October rain
the slag-heap sagged
its greedy belly.
He drew a picture of a wren,
his favourite bird for frailty
and determination. His eyes gleamed
as gorse-flowers do now
above the village.

His scream was stopped mid-flight.
Black and blemished
with the hill's sickness
he must have been,
like a child collier, dragged
out of one of Bute's mines.

There he is, climbing a tree,
mimicking an ape, calling out names
at classmates. Laughs springing
down the slope: my wife hears them,
ears attuned as a ewe's in lambing
and I try to foster the inscription,
away from its stubborn stone.

NIGEL JENKINS

To choose six poems, after two and a half decades' endeavour, that still seem to function: that was the first criterion. But there are other reasons, perhaps, why these particular efforts belong together, in spite of their seemingly disparate subjects, moods and approaches.

Much of what I have written, I now see, is born of a fusion of the personal and political, assisted frequently by a sense of history and place. The 'first place' was the family farm in Gower about which, after much trial and error, I wrote my first plausible poems; the mundane cruelties of a poem such as 'Castration' anticipate a more overt concern with the problem of human cruelty in poems such as 'Ainadamar' and 'Snowdrops'.

The poems of childhood led to an investigation of the family ('Yr Iaith', meaning the Welsh language) whose history drew me inexorably into a continuing engagement with my country's past and exasperating present. The alter ego of the pre-eminently Welsh poem of praise is the poem of dispraise and invective: satire has often been my response to the squalorous lows of recent political life, such as the vote against Devolution in 1979. 'Land of Song', I'm frequently told, is strident and vulgar; but if, as an irritant, it can do its tiny bit to culture the pearl of Independence (i.e. liberation from the British State into a more active relationship with the wider world), then I'll continue to lob it into crowded rugby clubs.

I don't write many poems about writing poems, an activity which can seem sometimes about as useful as plumbing for the sake of plumbing, but many of my offerings are incidentally, to varying degrees, poems about language, from the fate of one particular language ('Yr Iaith') to the universal difficulties of naming experience – or ('Shirts') failing to name it, encountering articulacy instead in the 'speech' of objects. I'm troubled too by the language of art, its viability: 'Can the poem?' asks 'Snowdrops'. I go on making poems in the hope that it can, but one's doubts increase. The poem loses strength as the language dies back, removing from the anglicized majority all but a trace of how once, here poetry played a central role in both the national polity and everyday life. I have a horror of poets writing only for other poets, and their academic pilot fish, which is why, I suppose, I don't bother much these days with literary magazines. Giving readings seems more important, and writing messages on walls: ambush.

Castration

Cutting, they called it –
but for all
his noise there was no
blood, no visible hurt:

just some thing in him
halted, to change
a bull-calf to a steer.

It didn't hurt, they said
as they caught and threw them,
locked each scrotum
for a second
in the cutter's iron gums.

The next one was mine:
round the yard we
chased him, brought him
down – hooves flying –
in a slither of dung.

They sat him upright,
like a man for barbering,
and I felt
in the warmth of his purse
for the tubes.
They gave me the tongs
and with all the steel
of my arms I
squeezed them home.

They fetched me another,
said he hadn't felt a thing.

But I wouldn't play.
With all that sky-wide bawling –
        sound his throat
        was never made for –
some nerve in me was severed.
There were words about
that weren't to be trusted.

Yr iaith

She who has forgotten
remembers as if yesterday
the scythe they left rusting
in the arms of an apple,
the final bang of the door
on those sheep-bitten hills.

In Abertawe, in Swansea
there were killings to be made,
and they politely made theirs.

She spent a lifetime loving
the taste of white bread, a lifetime
forgetting the loser's brown.
And on their middle floors
the brass gleamed, the crystal sang,
while away in the attic
dust fingered
the violins and the harp,
and far below stairs a discreet
and calloused tongue complained.

Years she remembers
of cuff-link and shoeshine,
but nothing, she says, nothing
of those dung-filled yards.

It's autumn now, an evening
that ends in colour t.v.
and the washing of dishes.
I ask her, as I dry,
Beth yw 'spoon' yn Gymraeg?
Llwy, she says, *llwy, dw i'n credu*,
and she bites into an apple
that tastes like home.

Land of Song

(I.m. 1.iii.79)

Oggy! Oggy! Oggy!
This is the music
of the Welsh machine
programmed – Oggy! – to sing
non-stop, and to think only
that it thinks it thinks
when it thinks in fact nothing.

Sing on, machine, sing
in your gents-only bar –
you need budge not an inch
to vanquish the foe,
to ravish again
the whore of your dreams,
to walk songful and proud
through the oggy oggy toyland
of Oggy Oggy Og.

Sing with the blinding hwyl
of it all: you are programmed
to sing: England expects –
my hen laid a haddock
and all that stuff.

Ar hyd y nos, ar hyd
y dydd – the songs, the songs,
the hymns and bloody arias
that churn from its mouth
like puked-up S.A. –
and not a word meant,
not a word understood
by the Welsh machine.

Oggy! Oggy! Oggy!
shame dressed as pride.
The thing's all mouth,
needs a generous boot
up its oggy oggy arse
before we're all of us sung
into oggy oggy silence.

Ainadamar

The Arab name for a fountain spring near Granada, where the Spanish poet Federico Garcia Lorca was murdered by Nationalist Fascists in 1936. The fountain, whose name means 'Fountain of Tears', used to supply water to the gypsy quarter of Granada.

'Comprendí que me habián asesínado'
— Federico Garcia Lorca.

Give him coffee, said the general,
    plenty of coffee:
and on the road from Viznar
to Alfacar the trees were silenced,
a leathern cloud muffled the voice
    of the moon.

It was cold, and all the world
    lay huddled in mist.
Hollow at heart, too tired to sleep,
he walked out through the dawn
to be alone with himself.
Give him coffee, said the general,
    plenty of coffee...
    In the white silence
not a leaf breathed, nothing moved
or was — until a gateway held him,
drew him in through portals of rust —
to take a seat among the weeds,
    among the statues
mouthing lost names to the leaves.

    Something there moved —
a lamb, perhaps, a tiny lamb
enkindled from the mist — and its
    movement warmed him.
Give him coffee, said the general.
    On she danced
by the dead statues, kicking dew
in their faces with her hooves of sunlight.
Coffee, said the general, black coffee:
and there burst upon the morning —
    hooves of rock,
    mouths of iron —

a gluttoned hoard of pigs
that tore at the lamb, that this
and that way ripped her like a rag
till they'd cleaned her, hoof and hide,
    from the world.

Give him coffee, said the general,
plug his arse with bullets
    for being a queer.

But on the road from Viznar
    to Alfacar
a creature of moonlight
is moving through the trees, is dancing
at the fountain of Ainadamar.
And the townspeople drink
    of singing water.

Shirts

She hangs out his shirts,
pins them by the tails
to the singing line.

She hangs out his shirts,
and in the pure green
that the lawn paints them
she can see her face:
I am his wife.

In the attention
of cushions, the soft
elisions of a door –
a voice, her voice
comes back to her:
he is my husband,
I am his wife.

I am the place
he returns to, his
hunger's home.
I build every day
a houseful of rooms,
of walls to enfold
the things that he loves.

She hangs out his shirts,
and the air they breathe
fills them with flight:
his gentle arms rage
flailing at the sky,
scratching and clawing
to catch up with the wind.

She hangs out his shirts:
he is her husband,
she is his wife.

Snowdrops

I know what I am doing here,

come every year
in the iron first month

to seek them out.

I choose my time,
a day to freeze
the waters of the eye,
and I move through it

– primal caver delving in sign –

to link with light
of the living blood.

*

Last year too soon,

not a white word
in all the wood's deadness.

Home then speechless

to wait.

*

Sky grey and lowering
curtains the wood:

no money, no food: hush
of alone here, cold
of hunger,

last place of warmth
a hole in the head
that's known, I remember, as mouth.

*

A man in a coat
hunting flowers.

Sudden scatty cackle –
the waving of a branch:
a magpie, I trust, has left the tree.

Here, now
the blue gift amazing
of kingfisher flight

would not be believed.
I ask only

snowdrops,
a warmer world.

*

A warmer world?

*

And here they nod
in the cold and quiet.

In Bolivia the soldiers
broke glass on the ground.
They made the naked children
lie flat on the glass,
they made the mothers walk
on the children's backs.

Here snowdrops nod
in the quiet and cold.

If the bomb fell on Swansea,
fifty miles away in Cardiff
eyeballs would melt...

Can
    a flower?
Can
    the poem?

*

Brother dead in Paviland:

the first I pick
I pick in celebration

of the species that stayed
when all others fled
the coming of the cold,

species now trembling
through a darker season
of its own manufacture.

*

Feet gone dead, hand around the stems
some borrowed thing, a clamp
of frozen meat

but

tlws yr eira

blodyn yr eira

cloch maban

eirlys

lili wen fach

– a song in my fist.

                *

The owl is with her
the day's length,
and she is sick
of the moon:

her winters are long.

I hand her snowdrops:
she grasps the primrose.

                *

Inside from the cold
they boast no bouquet,

just green breath
of the earth's first things.

I find them a glass,
and on the worktable
scattered with papers
I place them.

It is enough.

*

Thin sun creeps
upon the afternoon
and the water warms,
bubbles sprout
on the earthpale stems.

They'll die early, yes,
and drop no seed:

the year may live.

HUW JONES

I begin my selection with four poems dealing with decay and loss. The first takes a wry look at an old Austin being claimed by nature. 'The Tenth Visitor' was inspired by Causley's humorous poem 'Ten Types of Hospital Visitor' and the death of an old lady in hospital who had been a volunteer with me on the Aberystwyth League of Friends bus. My grandparents, who lived in Llanelltyd where I spent many happy childhood holidays, are the subjects of the next two poems. My grandfather died when I was nine and the memory of this time is expressed in 'Elegy'. After my grandmother's death I was reading through her old autograph book and then produced these snapshots of her life.

The next poems are reflections on life, its challenges and its joys. The poem 'Tirion Awel' is a celebration of the February birth of my second daughter in Llandrindod. 'Changing Roles' is the opening section of a longer poem about my daily life with her as a two-year-old. We changed roles when my wife was ordained into full time ministry. As a Nonconformist the performs the same duties as her male colleagues. In support of friends who are denied this opportunity in the Anglican Church I wrote 'Synod 1987'.

Also during this time we were active members in the peace movement and I wrote a number of poems about peacemaking of which 'Defence' is one. It looks at the mentality of certain people in their relationship with others. People's life-styles on a private housing estate where our manse is situated prompted a vision of the Keeper disturbing and even destroying the rich, sweet existence of its inhabitants in 'A Taste of Honey'.

As a bilingual person brought up in an anglicized part of mid-Wales and now living on Ynys Môn where Welsh is the day-to-day language of many in the community, my recent poetry in English and Welsh looks at the effects and the necessity of tourism for the economy and culture of Wales. A brochure by the Wales Tourist Board proclaiming Ynys Môn as 'Britain's Treasure Island' provoked me to write the poem of that title. The sight of Snowdon overlooking us and climbing its paths gave me the quirky idea of presenting the mountain's point of view.

The final poem comes from my continuing interest in artists. Lowry's later work often portrayed the lonely, isolated figure and after reading an account of his death in a biography I wrote 'Man Lying in a Hallway'.

Old Austin

Put out to grass,
abandoned for a faster breed
that races along motorways.
In the field's workshop
ferns slowly spray him green
rain refills the tank.

Some nights
when a bright moon
switches on his headlights,
a badger squats behind the wheel
and taxies home a few owls
tipsy after a barn dance.

The Tenth Visitor

'The tenth visitor
Is not usually named.'
        – Charles Causley

Quieter than others,
quieter than the night nurse
who doesn't notice him

striding down the ward
smelling of the cold night air.
He won't stay long.

He has come to move you.
it's quite official
and all will be taken care of.

Quieter than others
he takes infinite care
not to wake you up.

Elegy

It was the season when the trout
rise for the may-flies
as they skate along the Mawddach.

                        The house,
smelling of smoke and polish,
was full of strange aunts
sighing how tall I'd grown,
sipping their strong tea and tears.
It was my first death,
                        the house
dark and familiar, except for the large
coffin in the small parlour.

Too young to mourn
I ran down to the bridge
to watch the men fight with the fish,
cramming a jam-jar tight with tadpoles.

I have known other deaths,
but none so free.

Autograph Book 1918

This is my album
But learn 'ere you look
That all are expected
To add to my book.

After the Great War
coloured pages
of this Christmas gift
recorded quip and prayer
of relative and friend.

Jones for now
but not for ever –
a rash prediction
or a promise to a maid
leaving for London?

Take one pound of Resolution
two ounces of Experience
one large sprig of Time –
A recipe to cure
your lovesick heart.

May all your troubles
be little ones –
two daughters and a son
scattering hens in the yard,
pulling at your purse and apron strings.

Laugh and the world laughs with you.
snore and you sleep alone –
how the bed shook
with your snorting, the moon
grinning at the window.

Go, shut the leaves
and clasp the book –
your last signature
by the curling Mawddach
as it leaves the hills
for the open sea.

Tirion Awel

Now you are complete,
fingers soft as catkins
soon to be kissed
by winter sun,
your turning a token
of pain to come.

A crown of stars
and a silver moon
awaits your coming
out of darkness
as we with berry and thorn
adorn your Bethlehem.

You are gold
from the deep,
casket of flesh
from a secret cove

hauled at last
from the bones' rigging
you gasp for air
mouthe for comfort.

This is the night
of your nativity,
wrapped in my arms
your poverty I treasure.

For you, my daughter,
angels leave music
scored on window panes,
harps sparkling
on gutter and gate.

Above the Ithon,
choirs of beech
and blackthorn sing,
a parish of snowbells
proclaim the spring.

From *Changing Roles*

She is an alarm clock
always too early,
a mail train chuff-chuffing up the stairs
carrying letters from Postman Pat
shrieking with delight,
'Daddy, Jack Frost has been, come and see.'
The sheets are tugged away.

The musketeer leaves his chambers
puts on a brave face for the dawn duel
with a two-year-old
(not to mention his wife
who pretends to be asleep).
No need to slide down the banister today
to evade king's enemies brandishing swords,
he uses the stairs
switches on the central heating,
kettle, grill and radio.

'Railway workers kept the French train service crippled yesterday...'
    Harvest Crunch bounces into bowls.

'President Reagan laughed and joked with his doctors...'
    Smell of toast soon fills the kitchen.

'The Aids controversy took a dramatic new turn last night...'
    Eldest daughter plus Care Bear order breakfast for two.

'Singing superstar Aled Jones announced that he is to end
his brief career while it was on a high note...'
    Tea is sipped slowly as wine.

He steps into a wrestling ring
to dress the youngest
who runs around the ropes
avoiding vest, petticoat and frock.
Finally, pinned between his knees
the tats in her hair submit to a comb.

'The man said snow didn't he?'
The weather forecast is chanted with glee
as they trudge in wellies and duffle coats
towards the waiting spaceship,
wave goodbye and disappear
to a world of paper, paint and plasticine.

He drifts back to the autumn morning
when he stood by her bunk
after leaving her drowning
in someone else's arms.
He baked a batch of biscuits
to fill those first two hours
before carrying her home
knowing she would grow accustomed
to partings and reunions
in corridors and cloakrooms
as he released her slowly,
a kite in open country.

Synod 1987

'A little early to take the tarpaulins
off the lifeboats.' – Dr Robert Runcie

A little early to go
careering along the deck
tripping over cassocks
mitres rolling under rails?

As storm clouds threaten
and waves beat the boat
she wakes in the stern
to question your faith.

She has accepted your kisses
for centuries, jibes
and dirty jokes that are spit
in her face, bruises
that are nails in her soul.

Though you push her
to the back of your mind
how can she forget you
her breasts tingling with milk?

You've been living off her body
for years, breaking her
into tiny pieces with words,
abstractions of church and synod
burblings to her ears.

Stand back from the lifeboats.
Look, she is walking on the sea
drawing near to the boat
comforting a frightened crew.

Defence

He leans across the fence
cursing the start
of the lawn-mower season.
Armed with clippers and rake
he leaves his lawn
like a newly laid carpet
daffodils guarding the border.

Sipping beer on the patio,
broom resting on his knee
like a settler's shotgun,
he eyes with horror
fists of coiled fern
sprouting through a neighbour's hedge.

Between his fences
wild thoughts are weeded out
for perennial fear and prejudice
to flower in the mind's silo.

A Taste of Honey

No cry heralds his arrival
as he comes mid-afternoon
at the end of summer
when all is calm and warm.

He steps slowly over hill-tops
clothed in white boiler suit and gloves
trousers tucked into boots
and his face veiled by black net.

He stoops to a colony
of houses on a hill,
his smoker of old sacking
is stuffed at their doors.

Workers scurry over rockeries
mothers swarm to nurseries
as quietly and gently
he lifts each roof.

Some gorge themselves
in a last minute rush
before being brushed away
from their palaces of plenty.

Britain's Treasure Island

Welcome ashore, me hearties!
Escape the tide of modern life;
relax at award-winning inns
with four-poster bedrooms
and nautical bars.

Lamb is back on the menu
now Chernobyl's blown over
and recent leaks from Wylfa
are safely within limits.

Tour Goronwy's 'second Eden',
'Lady and mistress of the sea',
her rocky coves and sandy beaches
are monitored carefully.

I almost forgot,
at cromlech, castle, mill and mansion,
craft centre, pottery and maritime museum,
there's plenty to plunder
and X marks the spot.

View from Snowdon

You won't find a better place to live
or die, come to that. Travellers
from Giraldus to Tennyson
have raised their hats (and lost them)
to these remote turrets.
It was Pennant put me on the map
to be trampled and prodded by boot and crampon,
tempting painters for a scenic fix.
When the train came thumping up and down
I waved goodbye to privacy.

What do you hope to see up here,
Glyndŵr's eyrie, Arthur's lair?
Taskmasters have blurred your vision,
this is no climate for their return.
Can eggs be protected from determined collectors
or a language by law?

You are a people at the foot of Sinai
polishing a golden calf.
Tents outnumber sheep
second homes are worth a bomb
and even Rhita Gawr's garments
woven from the beards of dead kings
could be sold in the craft shops.

If I sound cynical, put it down
to old age. I'm tired of being
a refuge in your hour of need.
Judgement Day won't be as dramatic
as a cloudburst of rocks
but when the wind of tourism subsides
you will be left like stunted trees
in a bleak Reserve.

Man Lying in a Hallway

(L.S. Lowry, ten days before he died)

That morning
even his wireless was an irritation.
After lunch at the Alma Lodge
he'd snoozed away the afternoon
in his deep green chair. Then this:

fast to the floor like a sick dog
he lay where his knees had given way;
'Wait,' he cried, 'Wait,'
as a stream of chocolate biscuits
tumbled through the letterbox.

He listened to footsteps grow louder
then fade to a nearby bus-stop.
He threw his slippers at the door,
his diary, his wallet, then his watch.
No one came.

With darkness
weasel-faced callers
grinned behind frosted glass;
figures he'd pinned onto board
came tapping from the back room.

'Can you give me tuppence?' he cried
struggling to rise,
'Can you give me tuppence?'

STEPHEN KNIGHT

The world in my poems is full of dodgy footholds, vertiginous perspectives and slippery customers ill at ease in their surroundings. Like rented rooms, the stanzas are dotted with objects to make them more habitable. If I were to attempt a glossary, I might mention that my father is Anglo-Welsh, my mother Austrian (while I speak neither Welsh nor German) and that most of my poems have been written during protracted periods of unemployment; but if I knew what I wanted to say, I wouldn't be writing poems.

I had an inkling that this selection was, to a greater or lesser extent, addressing itself to the subject of Welshness, though I could be wrong. A few of the poems are set in specific locations – the three-quarters-finished Dylan Thomas Theatre in Swansea; the tall, thin building of my Comprehensive school – though as far as meaning is concerned, that's probably neither here nor there.

Mr Daymond, my A Level German teacher, once stopped a lesson on *Die Schwarze Spinne* by saying there was no point to literature any more – was there? – when all The Major Themes had been done: Love, Death, etc. Nobody challenged this provocative assertion and we went back to the book. I didn't know then that the point isn't *what* is said but *how* it is said, that it's important simply 'to be'.

Each generation discovers the world for the first time then tries to come to terms with it, to describe it in new ways. The subsequent novels, plays, poems settle like a geological stratum; each layer, each century, is different and yet basically the same.

I got an E for German.

A Species of Idleness

The rise in temperature wakes me now...
The bedclothes gather at my ankles.
Dressing, I check if the street is wet
for the first time in weeks: our window-
box is spiriting away the dregs
from the teapot like a colander.
My bedroom is a pigsty. Last night,
I slept on the ceiling with the moths.

My parents have been anchoring me
to furniture since the Fifth of June –
I spend the afternoons sunbathing
with a weight on my feet. My head still

rises up uncompromisingly.
The neighbours call me 'Dandelion'.
To cool myself, I lay my cheekbones
on our fat refrigerator door.

When a letter from Australia
arrives, it's taken to the kitchen
like a stack of dirty plates: I work
my way through the A4 sheets, clotted
with Tony's spidery hand. *Today,*
he writes, *I recorded the Outback –*
the clicking spokes of a bicycle,
the clack of hockey sticks from a field.

It's a bleak, vernal Sunday; the fish
in the river are counting their scales.
Your typewritten picture-postcards are
as cold as rubber gloves, and yet I
stand them on my desk and mantelpiece.
Have you no time to send a letter?
Food is never off my mind. Weightless
and bored, I feed on every page's

pieces of good advice: how to fill
the vacuum with games of patience
and botany – my hair is growing
faster than the grass (so I settle
for dry shampoo) and the king of clubs
reminds me of my two-faced father!
Despite my thorough shuffling, he
continues floating to the surface.

Every breeze disturbs me. I flicker
with the leaves and the pages of my
writing-pad like fire. Tending to drift,
I fill my pockets with stones and wear
a diver's metal boots, though they clash
with all my clothes. Tony recommends
fresh air and plenty of fruit. My skin
browns like bitten apple in the sun.

Double Writing

Sea View, Water's Edge, Atlantis,
lugubrious Guest Houses welcome the tide

after dark, from the opposite side of the road.
Their windows are lit with VACANCIES.

At closing time, Covelli's chips do a roaring trade
though his name has flaked from the side of the building.

Tighter than fists in the gaps in wooden benches,
pages of the local paper soak in vinegar.

Wind sizzles through trees
while, from the promenade, waves reach for the last bus

back into town. Ticking over in the back seat,
somebody sleeps it off. His thumb is in his mouth.

None of the timetables work
and graffiti spreads through the shelter like wires –

refinements of a thick, black autograph
above the spray of glass, below the one-armed clock.

In West Cross garages, drums, guitars and microphones
huddle together, waiting to be famous.

Things go quiet. Things are unplugged.
Cutlery is laid out for the morning.

Laughing Gas

I am timing the Fire Doors for something to do;
   they swing alarmingly! Since the Management reduced
our use of electricity, I walk the corridors
   trailing my fingertips the length of the wall.

   I think of adjectives to sum this building up:
   warrenous, *respectable* and *windowless*.
When you talk to me I watch the movement of your lungs,
   the ripple of the fibres of your mohair pullover.

   The mannerisms of our six close friends become
   as obvious as eyes: they fidget and tick like bombs.
You study their hands, their irritable hands and I,
   I make a note of everything you say and do.

   The time you spend on make-up is a blessing – your dead
   white cheeks are as good as light and heat to guide me
down the corridors! Concrete dust is rising from the floors
   like fire; when it reaches the lips it mixes

   with our exhalations. Temporarily, I believe
   in ghosts. Don't tell me that you don't!
Yesterday, your drawing-pad was open at a charcoal face
   wincing with a silly grin for want of oxygen.

Voyage to the Bottom of the Sea

The trick (he tells me) is to sleep till twelve
   then watch the television.
In the corner of his murky bedroom
   there is always a swirl of colour:

T-shirts; smoke threading from an ashtray
   to the light; shoes; anemones thriving
on the wreck of the Torrey Canyon;
   our Chancellor raising the Budget box.

Bedsitter Cookery

1

My room is a tunnel on the first floor:
the door at one end; a sink; a table;
the bed; then a window at the other.

The building hoards shadows through the summer
to hold them on my nostrils, mouth and eyes.
The smells of other tenants crowd the air.

Sharing the bathroom opposite my door
I discover trails of liquid footprints
and wafers of soap thin enough to post.

A soupçon of pubic hairs (three or four)
crops up in the tub, below the halo
of dirt. I have bought a bottle of Jif.

Buff envelopes from the DHSS
accumulate on the hallway table
beside the pay-phone, in the dark, like rice.

The ground floor kitchen bubbles with voices.
The cooker in the corner runs on gas.
The oven, at a pinch, can hold three heads.

2

Cooking smells rise
through my carpet
like moles;
I have an aerosol
for freshening
the atmosphere.
Yesterday
I met a tenant
on the landing
who assured me
that the house
is heated

by hot-water pipes.
– We talked about
our education,
his in Bath,
mine in a Swansea
Comprehensive:
five storeys,
all boys, sinking
in marshy ground,
year by year,
inch by plaster inch.
A teacher
was beaten up once
in a while,
but what on earth
made me mention that
I cannot say.

3

Cook the cauliflower
in a large saucepan
of boiling salted water
for 10 minutes or so,
until tender, then drain.
Meanwhile, put the cheese sauce mix
in a small saucepan,
stir in the milk and bring
to the boil.
Simmer for 2 minutes,
till the sauce has thickened,
stirring now and then.
Set it aside.
When eating, pour the sauce
over each floret
then sprinkle with parsley
(if using) and serve at once.

4

This is an all-male boarding house.
We stand, at night, in our separate rooms
at the mirror above the sink,
and masturbate. Cobwebs of semen
hang lazily in the plughole
till we wash them away; the plumbing
gargles and burps for a minute
then leaves the rooms in silence.

Stubble was seeping through his cheeks,
the cheeks of the man I chatted with.
Its plastic handle wound around
his fist, a Gateway bag hung
lumpy with food from the end of his arm.
I shall call them personal effects:
cheese; a loaf of bread; one pasty;
a carton of Um Bongo.

His sentences trailed like mutton...
I almost made a cup of tea
but electricity isn't cheap.
The meter by the bed consumes my cash
with the loveless voracity of sand;
my lights are fed.
I am barely twenty-five.
I deserve a better life.

5

The days, the weeks, the months
proceed like rain.
I walk on our suspension bridge
in a pair of trainers,
in a baggy jacket,
in a pair of denims,
in a shirt I change
several times a week,
in Y-fronts and socks.

I sprinkle something
other than parsley
onto the Avon
(a cupful of pebbles,
pigeon food –
something like money)
to make a wish,
a wish
for money.

Blue Skies

Following every storm
old photographs emerged like wings
from the bedroom, though nothing
could restore the calm

of years before, before they came to any harm –
turn-ups, a polka dot dress, one blustery day;
her arm hooked round his arm
as if that could stop him blowing away.

The Top Floor

Our bottled foetus
has flowering limbs,
I close the cupboard door
on it. In his room,
Mister Robins
is folding down
the thumbed corner
of a page of Milton,
loving the solid brickwork
of the verse.
I reach the top floor
panting;
a panatella

turns to dust
between his ochrous fingers.
In the yard, pupils
congregate like spawn:
a group of First Years
debate the size
of Barbra Streisand's breasts.
I lie
flat across the sill
and bellow to my friend
four floors below.
Looking up, he cups
his hands to his ears.
Angelic and bald,
our bottled foetus
wallows in stasis
as vowels and consonants
fall like sediment.

Towards a Definition of Heaven

I watch the whole house watching me: eight solid rooms.
Here is our deep blue living-room carpet,
lapping the skirting board with threads. His photographs are up.
I sink in the sofa; its concave cushions
hold their dusty breath a little tighter for me.

An unread column of library books
trembles like a fish when I turn the television down.
Faces bob across the screen, buoyed up by pairs of
grey, substantial shoulders. Last week, he was balanced
on the edge of his chair to catch the punchlines.

Today, now, his trousers and his best white shirt
swoon beside the castors. On the antimacassar,
slivers of him coagulate; slower, by far, than grease.
The weather forecast is on: his all-time favourite,
you tell me as you pour the coffee.

As intangible as isobars and swimming in
soft focus, your portrait looks reproachfully
on us – on your rationing me to a level teaspoon
of sugar. I inherit his sweet-tooth,
his books and his recipe for making wine.

Seeing the splashes on your tipsy rubber plant,
I recollect our telephone conversation:
his goitre, you still insist, dripped through his collar;
a tear streamed; and then his whole face streamed; his vital organs
beached on the rug when he hit the blue,

blunt carpet head-first, splashing, yes, the rubber plant...
We'll wipe these incrustations off this afternoon,
before the sun slants in to gild what's left of him.
(I think of a pink meniscus now: chattering with heat
and light and dust; tense before it falls.)

At the Foot of Division Four

Ow footbawlTeem wares blackenwhite:
a angz a reds, a looks kuntrite
fuhlOozin, Homer N'weigh,
buhstill aisle go unwatchum-play
in Winter wenner Windsor blowin
9gaylz offaSee unthrowin
rubbish rowndee airmTee stanz,
blowin ice throo my airmTee ands.

John Toshack wozzer-marrNidjer-wenn
a roe-zupp 2 Division won.
Enner sighed wasFuller codjers
attee-endov Ayr Koreas;
e boreTum fuhPeenutz neigh played
foruh season. Nunnervumstaid,
uh-gnat wozzer long thymer go.
Now we backin Division Phaw!

Prap zitzer clymitt aura food
innease parts duzzEwe so muchgood
eye-dun-owe, buttie oldest laydee
inner Brittish Aisles livzbuymee,
innerGnome. Givvortayker year
ov breethin Saul tea Swornzee Heir
sheezer nundruden-nighn, unTV
filmzer birthdaze rare gullully.

Sheezlimp, tie-udd, uvairj Tubble:
ur riser bearLeigh vizzible
re-seedin inner-red: ur skinz
udared, crakt Riverbared nuthinz
swammerbuv frayJiz: wenner voyss
leex throo gapZinnerShrungkunFayce
shee sairz sodAwl turimEmber
(lyke pose cards senTin Dissember,

nuthin air Butter Sea nurry).
Air vreethin z'owld innis cuntree –
gray ills, gray treez Anna poe-stuh
s'been stuckon Neath stayshun frair-vuh:
iss flew-rare-sunt unrareLidjuss
wither quaresChunn inbiggLairtuzz,
aniss quaresChunn tare-riff-eyes me.
Where will YOU spend Eternity?

HILARY LLEWELLYN-WILLIAMS

I was on the other side of the world, in the middle of the southern summer, thinking of winter in Wales, when I selected these poems. Being half a world away from the place where I'd written them lent them some distance and helped me to be objective. Here were poems from a faraway land and another time: I would never write in that way here. Sitting with the contents of my file scattered around me, I found the final choice reflecting my mood; taking stock of the past few years before embarking on the rest of my life.

I arranged my choice as I might arrange a reading: partly intuitively, poems that seemed to work well together; partly deliberately, mixing reassuring old favourites with a few surprises to stop anyone falling asleep. I began with 'The Trespasser' as the poem that has become my hallmark at readings: if I don't read it someone will inevitably request it. It's a good opener here, and perhaps typical of my subject-matter and style.

'The Little Cloth' is a less predictable choice, but important as a personal statement. I spent years rejecting my Catholic upbringing only to discover its influence in shaping the kind of poet I am. The poem attempts to reconcile my past and present beliefs with a celebration of passage into adult womanhood – a process that is probably not complete yet.

'Andarax' links my Welsh and Spanish heritage, and is also a reminder to return to my grandfather's native country someday. 'Candlemas' is particularly personal, being in memory of my father; but it's here for his sake, and for my family, and for others who have told me they like it.

I included 'The Bee-Flight' partly because of its optimism and positive vision, and partly as a fair expression of my attitude towards landscape and seasons. 'Holly', from "The Tree Calendar", is in a similar vein and is representative of the sequence, though it reads well enough on its own.

'Alchemy' and 'Athene' are from a very different sequence of poems, inspired by Renaissance thought and magic. 'Alchemy', appropriately enough, grew alchemically from a vague and small idea to a statement of central importance to that collection. I nearly didn't include 'Athene' because of its length, but felt it deserved a place if only for its female-oriented view of human culture and spirit which is basic to my outlook, underlying practically everything I write. The 'little monk', by the way, is Giordano Bruno, chief protagonist of the poems.

I have closed with 'Brynberllan', about the village in Dyfed that was my home for seven years. The poem conveys something of my feeling about place, time and destiny; and also the *hiraeth* that is inescapable for anyone who lives in and loves this part of Wales.

The Trespasser

My fingers are sweet with stealing
blackcurrants. Among tall weeds
ropes of them, thick and ripe like secrets.
I move in shadow, sharpeyed, listening.
A distant car sets my spine quivering.
Bold as a bird I pull the berries down,
gather them in. Their smell excites me.

The house is blind: no one is living here,
yet I am trespassing. Each summer the owners
come for a week or two, cut grass,
clean windows, stare out from their gate.
But the river sings all year; and swifts make
nests, flowers bloom and fruit
ripens, and snow sweeps the lawn
smooth for the prints of foxes.

In spring there were daffodils, massed gold
and white narcissi; I ran in the rain
to gather armfuls, carrying them home
to shine in my windows. I live by here
every day, in poverty. What the hedges grow,
what's in the hills, I take back for my children.

Great polished blackcurrants in my fist.
They drop in the bag, grow fat.
Tonight I'll mix them with sugar, and steam
them slowly. The dark, sour, smoky taste;
my children's red mouths and chins,
their high, bird voices. Each year the trees
step forward round the house: I notice that.
In the autumn, I'll come for apples.

The Little Cloth

The odour of sanctity. Candles
their clear warm waxy spirits,
fresh cut blooms in paschal yellows and white,
bitter incense swung by a solemn boy,
the smell of washed Sunday bodies.

I was fifteen: I had waited a long time.

I knelt between mother and sister.
The priest moved his hands like a doll
decked out in ivory and gold for Easter.
Latin today: charmed occult syllables
long rustling silences, the soft chink of censers,
altar boys, white lace, male mysteries.

Sleepily I watched my own candle dip
and shrink in its fiery terrace
under the virgin's peeling plaster toes.
I hugged an unusual dragging ache, a tightness.

Sometimes I thought I might become a saint
to go into ecstasy and talk with angels;
not worry about my figure, my crop of spots
but to live in a forest hut on wild herbs
breathing wisdom like clean air.

The bell's small icy note
startled me back: the white moon
of the host raised up, then the chalice.
This is my blood, he said, and drank,
and wiped the cup. When that cloth is washed
(a priest once told me) the woman
must be in a state of grace
and the water not tipped down the sink
but emptied on the ground – just think of it.

My grandmother washed and washed little bloody cloths.

Ecce Panis Angelorum a woman sang
from the choir, her voice sexless and pure.
Strong vowels responded: I felt a loosing

of knots, a moist unfolding
from darkness, my chalice filled with blood

and the gold eyes of every angel turned
towards me, and I burned
with sudden grace, and my moon-Jesus rose
from the shadows and saw me. I was a saint at last –
my blood poured out for you
and for many; my new huge pride.

The soft white secret cloth
between my legs, reminded me all day.

Andarax

(Almeria, Andalusia)

On the map, a broad blue sinuous line said
water. Dark, fluid and cool
from the snows of Sierra Nevada,
bordered by orange groves and thirsty vines
threading and falling, a ripple between banks

because in Wales a river means moving water
I pictured that. So nothing prepared me for
nothing – that yawning ditch of dust,
that void, that absence. Sun spat
and crackled in the stones. Baked mud

cracked open. A long bridge spanned
the gulf. Everything the bleached-out dun
of old shit. On a ruinous site nearby
a JCB dug slowly: the dust went ten feet down –
further, the whole way. Crossing the no-river,

crossing the Andarax, I shuddered; my throat
dry as a lizard's, my eyes peeled raw.
Down to bedrock. Even its name's a cough,
a rasp, a drought. It does not summon liquid,
shadowy pools, slack shallows, slide of fish.

It's the name of a slaughtered dragon;
a mythical beast; a fossil; a chained Book
of Spells, with dark parchment pages: *Andarax*.
Somebody mentioned a winter legend of water,
snow-floods. I could not believe it:

that was too long ago, in another country.

The Bee-Flight

That was a strange, rare place, in a loop
between river and nippled hill
with a crooked sandstone church and trees
that corkscrewed, and a massive leaning yew
one thousand years thick, peeled rosy flesh
and a woman carved into the north wall
with legs agape, and a man with a bird's head
whistling sorcery. The ground rose
in hummocks: the past, carelessly buried,
trying to break through. Snowdrops showed white
and wet below the mound. I stood at the cusp
of spring in a flayed landscape
bleached-out by frost, stripped clean

as an old bone, sucked dry. I'd thought
there was nothing to fill me, nothing to speak to me;
but here was rain smelling of turned earth,
the sun in watercolour, curved paths,
storybook trees, bark swirled, bulged-out and fissured
peopling the place. At the edge of a pool
a straddled oak with a hole
at eye level, forced me to stare. Birds calling, then
a humming past my ear, and again; brown bees
sailing in from the sedges, dipping down
into darkness, hollow mouth-oak, in and in
with grains of new gold. A ragged shower blew
up from the west. Something unfolding, stirring

under my feet. The lumpy, breast-topped crag
now spiralled in light; the birdman suddenly answered
by choruses of wings, and the opened thighs
of the sandstone witch by the presence of flying bees.

Holly

Here in high summer, holly sets fruit
that will redden come Christmas.
Its prickles gloss and crackle in the sun.
Those deathless leaves make holly king.

This tree is holy, but not kind. What
is this holiness? What gift of grace
is so sharp-edged, dark-branched, hedged
with superstition, crowned with thorn?

Last summer's holly scratched my small
son as he climbed a bank, from rib
to breastbone a long stripe, with beads
of berry-blood, a flaxen Christ, arms up

and crying. This summer's rain
has blighted our best crops; but the trees
thrive, the trees take precedence. Green
under grey skies: reign of wood and water.

As the days shorten, holly's power grows:
ripening power, the birth power, power
from behind the eyes, dream power, spear-
leaved and bitter-barked and full of berries.

Holly saplings under graveyard yews
like prongs of resurrection, spring
from the shadows. The yews red-fleshed
and folded secretly, gave birth to them.

Blood mixed with soil was the old way
harvests grew fat, and holly ruled the feast.
My torn child heals: a ragged silver line
across his breast, fades as he flourishes.

Candlemas

On Brigid's Night
there was rain and wind and miles of darkness between us:
there was a generation of pain between us,
but I stayed awake for love's sake, and because of the candles.

On Brigid's night
spring was calling a long way off, below the horizon
invisible, but heard, like a changed note:
my ears attuned, I lit candles around the room.

My children slept
upstairs, bundles of summer. I was tight-strung
and humming. Nineteen points of fire
in a small room needed watching; I sat with them.

My eyes half-closed
I watched them burn all night, watched wax spill pools
and curl and flow, the flames dip low,
wrapped round in shadows, caught in the eye of light.

The night you died
I talked to you through webs of sleep, recalling
you in my years of childhood
solid and sure, filling the fiery spaces.

I slept at last
towards dawn, in a darkened room. Slowly I woke
to sunlight striping the carpet, the cold
little heaps of wax: and my children shouting, and spring

one day nearer
and bottles clanking outside, and a sense of peace
and freedom; then the shrill cry
of the telephone, which I stumbled up to answer.

Alchemy

We are in a state of continual transformation:
fresh atoms are continually being reincorporated
in us, while others that we received beforehand
escape from us.   (*De l'Infinito*)

Wonderful what will come out of darkness:
stars, owl voices, sleep;

water, green shoots, birds' eggs
with their own curved darkness;

gemstones; a whole and perfect child
from my unseen recesses; delight

from behind shut lids, finding each other,
fingers and tongues made delicate by night.

Great magic's performed after sunset.

Old alchemists conjuring angels,
witches dancing spirals under the moon;

drum-shamans, their spirit journeys;
three nights in a tomb

staging a resurrection. Transformations
taking place out of ordinary sight.

Daylight gives us boundaries, fixes
everything. The world separates
into colours and chemicals, figures
and faces. Surfaces appear solid
reliable, unconfused. We can see
to operate complex machinery.
Only darkness permits mixing

of elements, stirring of essences
in secret, combing dark and bright

into new patterns while we sleep; so dawn
finds us transformed, shifted.

Star-particles link us with trees
dolphins and stones, travel through us

creating the universe. Base matter

becomes gold: in the Cauldron
of Annwn, in the crucible of mind

we're all magicians. The Hidden Stone,
Elixir of Life, eludes us; we've lost

the art of working through touch
with invisible forces: but as darkness

rises, and we grope wildly, perhaps
out of chaos the magic will come right.

Athene

Her have I loved and sought from my youth, and
desired for my spouse, and have become a lover of
her form... and I prayed... that she might be sent
to abide with me, that I might know what I lacked
... for she knew and understood...
  (*Oratio Valedictoria*)

First, they made me an eye.
In the cold revolving stars, in the storm,
in the flying sun, in the place where water
comes out of the earth, an eye.
The eye watched; they were not alone.
They scratched its shape on stones
where the dead lay. Its rays spun out
weblike, encompassing the world;
drilled into bone, a passage, a way through.

Next, they made me a brow.
Over two staring circles, a double bow,
thick plunging curves, a look
of intense concentration. Life

with some thought behind it, an intelligence.
By now, they'd invented pots:
comfortable pregnant bellies, with twin eyes
frowning out of the clay. Sense
out of nonsense. Room to grow.

Then came the owl: that was natural.
Something alive and searching after dark –
that great dished listening face.
Soundless flight; wings a whisper of snow,
then the sudden swoop of death.
The voice of a world both fearful and beautiful
was a shuddering *hoo, hoo*. That suited me.
I flew secretly; I stunned, I wooed,
I tore apart, I saw and heard all.

And lastly, a woman born
out of sea-foam, out of flowers, or from
the head of a god – ridiculous. I'd been
too generous: the people thought too much;
they gorged on metaphors, they killed for them.
I was Athene, wise and terrible
flinging my spears, helmeted with the Moon,
crowned with stars, a woman clothed with the Sun
defending Right and Might and Truth and Freedom.

But now, little monk, by dusk
I see you kneeling on the cold flags
of your narrow cell, and your mind
is all eyes. In your heart a dark fire,
a lust. You have trusted me
and I have come: but I will not come kind
or maidenly – never forget, I am taloned,
banished from daylight, savage with desire –
but beautiful, yes my love; and I see, I see.

Brynberllan

This is a place where nothing really grows
but water: water and stones.

And concrete bungalows, and lost holdings.

Tilt of water from the mountainside
pushes under the road, and stones grow
overnight in our gardens: rainbuffed hard
perennials. We're on the flank
of the wind, even in summer.

But years ago, this was an apple orchard.

Rows and patterns of trees, all the way
down to the stream called *Comely*;
mossy barked, their darkblue stems at dusk,
the sun spread white at dawn on slopes
of blossom; warm air, stirred thick
with honey. Humming and swarms, and then
the smell of ripe fruit: those small
sharp western apples.

Crowded faces, bushels and basketfuls.

Everyone there, at work in the branches,
measuring the loads, brownarmed
and busy. Shouts in the crisp leaves.
Children rolling windfalls down the hill.
Foxes nosing at night through bruised grass.

And apple smoking in the soul-fires.

I think the traffic worsens year by year
just passing through. Rain's harsher too:
laced with acid and caesium, it fills
the stream called *Comely* and the stream
called *Blossom*. Nothing flourishes.

Yet sometimes we'll distill, between breath

and breath, a taste of sweetness:
yes, even now, a rustling of leaves
a blossom-drift. Between low flakes
of October sunlight, treeshapes flicker;
and evenings to the West bring cloud-landscapes
rising like a range of wooded hills,
a place of apple-orchards. Not here: beyond

reach, elsewhere, forsaken, forfeited.

CHRISTOPHER MEREDITH

These poems were written between about 1980 and 1989. They aren't arranged chronologically.

The background of a few pieces may be of interest.

'On his photograph outdoors' came to be written when I – among others – was approached by an art student who wanted to take my photo and then superimpose some of my words on the image. The poem was a response to the picture and eventually became the superimposed words. I was pleased to get a pun out of the word 'On'.

'Intricate May' is a free translation of a medieval Welsh poem. I originally did the piece to be a part of my second novel and took liberties with the text accordingly – even cutting three lines from it – but I was smug enough about the result to want to let it stand on its own. A much closer translation of the same poem is in Tony Conran's *Welsh Verse* under the title 'Sadness in Springtime'.

What goes on in making a poem is more like exploring than declaring. I don't want to graft the manifestos of hindsight onto this partly mysterious process, so I've made this selection according to no particular principle or intention. I would have liked to include one or two longer pieces but, in the economics of anthological space, a series of shorter poems probably gives better value.

Desk

I rescued you, splinted your broken legs.
Forty years or so had scummed you dark
With ink, dead skin, the rain of dust, the grease
Of knees and cuffs and fingertips, with work

Done routinely by the bored but paid.
I unlidded you, cut wedges, made true
The skewed split joints, machined human gluten
Off the boards. My carpentry of nails and glue

Fell short of craft but was informed by love.
I plugged you, cleaned your handles, planed,
Saw purity of copper and the packed white grain.
Some wounds were healed, the depth of others learned

– No restoration ever is complete.
People at work, the children and the staff,
Gave you their own disfigurement –
Not inborn malice but the hurt of graft

That rubbed a hole in their humanity.
And I played samaritan out of guilt
Of sorts. Worked out, I was looking for my
Small re-creation as you were rebuilt.

Relidded, drawers eased, your eight legs firm,
Beeswax bringing alive the fans and bars
Of tan and yellow grain, you are a place
For another sort of work. We're both scarred

But the worm in each of us is dead.
I'm not paid much, but neither am I bored
Nor hurt by work's attrition as we go
To real work. This page, the silence, these words.

From *Six Poems for Troedrhiwgwair*

Uncle Billy in the front room

Lemon- and biscuit-coloured light.
The oilcloth under the highframed bed
dusted clean, lightflooded
and me and my younger brother
shy children with the invalid.

We would like a bed pushed in the sun,
a frame like that to keep the blankets
off our legs.

He laughs and makes us exercise,
pedal air. Keep fit, he says.

But this is something absolute and good
and 'uncle' no relation, just his name.
The shrunken man, unshaven, spectacled, thin,
is misread as permanent.
Uncle Billy ambered in light and memory.

So fine to be tubercular like this:
a room with a bed,
a suntrapped, latticed bookcase.

Fixed in light on
a bookspine of a tale of castaways
a hero clambers an exotic hill.

Taking my mother to Troed

We saunter along both the rows
And at each door she names a ghost,
The family history and how
They died, or moved, or why they stayed.
Rob Roberts her father, Auntie Ada,
Pen Rogers, George Wimblett like a
Daicapped christ heaving firewood,
Mason's Farm, The Woods, New Pits.
Naming of the haunts and haunters
Somehow fixes things, though names
Like colours come loose in the dark.

On top row a bus turns, empty.
From grass erupting through the tar,
The burnt-out school, the breezeblocked doors,
She looks up to the breaking hill.
'Oh good god, o' course it've moved.'
She wonders at the few who've stayed,
Says she would not go back to this. So
Sadness would be affectation
Making us the passing tourists
Eager to be sentimental
About sheepshit, empty buildings.

Larks

Snow retracts in hollows
Above the adit mouth which
Blows rank air under larks climbing.

Houses without people
Lose all sense of self-respect:
Mosses etch the mortar, slates fall

And plaster falls from laths.
The piebald hill shrugs off snow,
Shrugs off people and the walls

Give up and tumble. Cars
Come and callers sup the past
And leave. To give up and be sad,

Like stones, is so easy
Though this is scarcely even sad –
Just random, as where weeds will grow.

Like winddriven midges
We came, clung a moment, went
When economics belched up the drift

With the reek of fear.
Matter is so unheeding
Blame needn't taint the taste of loss.

Yet over Troedrhiwgwair
Larks nail light with hammered air
Climbing, will-sustained, beyond sight.

The Vegetable Patch

Every year I turn it over, reluctantly.
The levered spade turns up treasure.
Pink spidery flowers on a plate-lip
Not enough to tell the whole pattern.
A ridged shard. The foot of a saucer, perhaps.
Earthenware a finger thick
Suggests a pantry-slab, stored ale.
The levered spade turns up the dead:
A clay-pipe stem like bone, the marrow sucked,
Thin Victorian china for bits of skull.

Our shelves inside are filled with
Complete sets, in use, neatly arranged.
Sometimes I wonder what we'll leave,
Or whether I'll ever, turning
The blade like this, find all the bits
Of just one plate from some old dresser.
But mostly I wonder whether, this year,
It should be lettuces or spuds.

On his photograph outdoors

Who does he think he kids?
He doesn't belong in this and will, soon,
be back in his house on the main road
– so many nozzles on a sewer – consuming
processed cheese and televised snooker.

The place has become less itself
than a space to visit in.
A child's voice fills a moment in the field,
is bloomed with far off silences
or the indifference of traffic sounds.

It has become less itself than a place
where words slip round the nearest tree.
Sometimes he finds their prints
and makes a few blurred plaster casts,
though no one can make much of what they are.

So the poem's a kind of inner sasquatch,
half mocked, only finding credence among
isolated children, like himself.

The world's another planet we explore
in zipped suits, enduring its poison air.
Home's a smudgy nebula within,
light years away, exploded ages since.

A Waiting-room

After midnight, fill another glass.
Today will just be more of the same.
More seed in the palm no longer seen,
great dawns joining all the rest
in the cellar with sunsets, misty mornings.
Blushing gets harder. Embarrassment
like pain will go at last.
You know I once held Epicurus strong
and once as well I was adored.
When that stops it makes no odds
if Epicurus was right or wrong.
However much it's fun, you're bored.
All making taints itself with this:
the fear of only being.
Action and praise like Sunday hymns
are the vapour-trail of what's important
or the crumby magazines we read
as we shuffle bums along a bench
towards the door of the waiting-room.
The song, the carpentry, the seed,
after the end of true delight,
are habits that affirm or ease
the rolling by of day and night.

1985

I met a friend.
I've been on strike, he said.
One year and then we lost. Cops
held me for a bit then let me go.
But I was innocent see.

I met a friend.
I've been away, he said.
They said I had a bomb. Remand.
One year. Then they let me go.
But I was innocent see.

And my friends said,
I know it was not what I did
it was not for the things I did
that they took me.
What I think and what I represent
are what they hate –
the blame's in what I am, not what I do.

And friend, since you call us friend,
where were you?

Jets

All day the jets have rifled through the air,
Drilled through the lessons that I've tried to give,
Scabbing the blue with vapour for a scar,
Passing the dummy-bombed hamlets with a wave.

I've comforted myself. I'm not so bad,
I've thought, in spite of the raised voice, the sudden squall
If discipline and strictness knocks them dead
At least I'm not out there learning to kill.

And each frail cliché rears to the surface,
Writhes in the strong light, dies, and having sunk
Leaves me to know I work for who in office
Shuts books to put more octane in the tank.

What *I* would does not possess our minds.
This boy, the fat one, has been rifled too.
Belongs to the plane and every bomb it sends,
Absorption melted from his ragged row

Of words. Just now he, my bluntest blade
Inevitably felled first in any game,
Looked from the tortured page, the word-wrought board,
To a sky where steel hammered its own scream –
And smiled.

Intricate May

After a medieval Welsh fragment

Intricate May the loveliest month.
   Birds' clangour. Branches writhe and wind.
The ox in yoke. Ploughs rutting earth.
   Green ocean and the mottled land.

When cuckoos call on greening trees
   Grief hurts the worst.
Smoke in the eye, long sleeplessness
   For kinsmen lost.

Endings

Bits of scorched lung clog the bronchia.
No air to brighten the blood, his brain fades
And he watches as from miles away
The panic floating round him silently –
Figures reaching for the phone, nervous fingers
Twitching the collar loose, the desperate
Remote thump on the chest – and all the time
The muffed boom of a heart that needlessly
Pumps the spent blood.

Waking in the quiet after the rush
To the machined valve of the airbottle
And a clock that ticks only on its face
He sees cool clouds soothing the window.
Neither industry nor cigarettes can
Worry us. Blame is not the subject. Think
How gardens drape the tips, tree-roots lace them
And how what's known outside is well-kept park.
Inside the heart like a continent needs
More world than the duty of relatives,
The small precisions of a watchful nurse
For the well of memories and pain still raw
Like a slaughtered whale turning on the surface.
Yet calm is more than what's most easing.

That moment when the flesh cools under
The bleak familiar bedroom ceiling
Should have all the heat of what's hardest said,
Like, say, *love* and *reconciliation*.
From miles away the world is frozen blue
But there are passages like flame or blood.
Across the planet Africa is sprawled
Burning under ice. The still head on the
Pillow knows more of that than the smoothed sheet,
The cold that crawls by fractions in the pipe
– So we need no further recognition.
We watch the glitter of a shoal of birds
Switching direction in the valley.

Christening pot boiler

Chamber maid
or cabin boy
passenger
room taker
true squatter
womb liner
woman filler
menses stopper
vomit causer
quasi modo
crouched at bellmouth
belly burden
bone garden
meat tumulus
homunculus
extra pulse
fish fellow
flesh hoop
human coil
vein labyrinth
amnionaut
tethered selky
potence prover
cash remover

accident-
al occupant
multiplication
and addition
love's dower
placenta flower
blanket denter
bladder squasher
snug dweller
dug sweller
milk maker
udder flooder
tum tickler
mother kicker
sleep spoiler
pot boiler
caul crammer
wind jammer
blood swimmer
gore surfer
dam buster
home breaker
mess maker
distraught squaller
future crawler,
welcome.

Monsters

Cardboard-headed
I lumber on the lawn
searching all its angles for my son
and *beepo* it's his turn.

He puts the box on.
A two-foot zombie chases me
but soon gets tired, prefers
to be pursued, cackles while he runs, though
there's no escape on this cramped patch of green.

My turn again.
Inside, soft light penetrates
the cardboard's subtle buff
and intimate as the smell of binding
on a close-held book comes
the whiff of apples that once packed the box
far off
glimpsed like something gleaming in deep water.

The monster stops, tasting.

We take turns to play him, to know
the cramps and music of our island.

Forked Tree

Sap's squeezed from heartwood
in our thickened trunks.
We're two on one root, though
we've leant away in growing
this age past.

There's sunlight sometimes.
Live things come and pester us,
call, flit.
We gesture something close to love,
make them high cradles,
think perhaps they answer our *why*.

When crowns begin to break at last
they'll go for good.

Stretching few leaves we'll
keep the quiet, feel bone whiten,
knowing as we always did
that we lead nowhere except back
to our one self.

ROBERT MINHINNICK

Asking myself why I have selected these poems, I suppose one of the answers is that they clearly link two of the themes that reoccur in my work: a sense of fear, and a need to celebrate. They might, in a modest way, be said to deal with the irreducible strangeness of the world.

Never trust the familiar, might be a by-word for these poems. At least never doubt that it conceals the extraordinary. I might even say the alien. When I think of the writing I see pictures. A motorway closed by snow, a house glimpsed across a lake, a loft, a country whose devastated ecology matched its political bankruptcy. (How easy, looking at 'In the Watchtower' now, to pretend that I foresaw the collapse of Czechoslovakia's communist regime as being as inevitable as the uprooting of one of its acid-rain-damaged trees.)

Fear and celebration, yes. But also I write about survivors. The young men in 'Yops' scared me, but their appetite for life was rarely less than exhilarating. Likewise the men and women of 'The Looters', nameless, mere shadows, who took advantage of a snowstorm to restock their larders and wardrobes. They are in a way my people, although the act of writing about them inevitably describes the gulf between us.

If I had to make a selection of poems tomorrow I might choose a different nine. But this work, it is almost painful to say, so bare does it look on the page, contains fairly constant concerns. I write about fairgrounds and dunelands and ugly, quiet towns; and the people in those places, some of whom might be the ugly, quiet heroes we pass everyday in the street. I hope there is no sentimentality in this writing. I am told sometimes that there is obscurity. Anyway, what links the poems, is the energy I found to write them, a feeling of pure excitement and determination which I hope is communicated. If it is not, then the work fails. I don't write for therapy's sake.

As to the connections between these pieces, those are for the reader to make. But for me the man who peers into the snow-infested attic, the soldier who stares out at the spruce forest from the watchtower, the couples in the museum of horror, the boys burning their names on to a table, are all looking for and at something. They are trying to make sense of things and not entirely failing. I can recognize myself in all those people. Which is perhaps one of the great discoveries of poetry. At least for the writer.

The House

I lie across the rafters of the loft
Holding the torch. From the junction box
Wires twist into darkness, a crumbling
Skein of red and black under sackcloth
Of webs. For three stifling hours

In the attic's heat I have cursed
This challenge, frustrated by
Electricity – the merciless current
That will not come. And the silence
Of the house offers no clue. Matching

Myself against its fifty years,
The solid rooms and gables of this redbrick
Terrace, I must establish my own
Permanence. For territory is not
Bought or sold but fought over: it is

The first instinct, the small, unremarkable
Warfare of our lives. Yet crouched in this
Hot attic room my sweat has turned to ice.
The torchbeam's yellow cylinder
Identifies the dust, shapes from life

That have served their time and been abandoned
By the house. And I stare, fascinated,
At the dead. The faces of those who once called
This house home. Like them, like this frail
Blade of light, the house has swallowed me.

The Drinking Art

The altar of glasses behind the bar
Diminishes our talk. As if in church
The solitary men who come here
Slide to the edges of each black
Polished bench and stare at their hands.
    The landlord keeps his own counsel.

This window shows a rose and anchor
Like a sailor's tattoo embellished
In stained glass, allows only the vaguest
Illumination of floor and ceiling,
The tawny froth the pumps sometimes spew.
    And the silence settles. The silence settles

Like the yellow pinpoints of yeast
Falling through my beer, the bitter
That has built the redbrick
Into the faces of these few customers,
Lonely practitioners of the drinking art.
   Ashtrays, a slop-bucket, the fetid

   Shed-urinal, all this I wondered at,
Running errands to the back-doors of pubs,
Woodbines and empty bottles in my hands.
Never become a drinking-man, my
Grandmother warned, remembering Merthyr
   And the Spanish foundrymen

   Puking their guts up in the dirt streets,
The Irish running from the furnaces
To crowd their paymaster into a tavern,
Leather bags of sovereigns bouncing on his thigh.
But it is calmer here, more subtly dangerous.
   This afternoon is a suspension of life

   I learn to enjoy. But now
The towel goes over the taps and I feel
The dregs in my throat. A truce has ended
And the clocks start again. Sunlight
Leaps out of the street. In his shrine of glass
   The landlord is wringing our lives dry.

Yops

       It waits for them
In the shadow, the rainsmoke.
The pines' blue quills
Sweep over it, and roof pitch
Blinks with all its lizards' eyes.
Then daylight turns its huge key
In the lock.

The shed fills up with fizzing smells and words.

The tabletop's burnt with their names
For each other, the scorched identities
Of this year's clutch of teenaged working men

Kicking the clodges round
In parched boots bracketed with lime
And studs like quillets, their brutal jewellery.
Through denim shreds move the cartoons
Of last year's loves and hates.

Over picks and mattocks
They push inside.
Over green cement dust frozen into ribs across the floor
They warm themselves on language hot as rum.

Wait an hour.
Feel the moods erupt, dissolve. Twitching
Like lurchers they face a world framed by a door
And walls where girls are starfish,
Sulky eels.

Low as rainsmoke, thermos-steam
The great frustrations hang.
Steelies start to tap the leaking boards.

'The Kingdom of Evil'

Afraid of the dark, of being alone,
We come here to investigate
The cause of our unease, the root of a fear
That's a common bond; our inheritance.

Heads torn from bodies, limbs with the pale
Glimmer of fungi; and under glass
A simple and ingenious device
For causing as much possible pain

To a human being. The technology
Is plausible but the terror lies elsewhere.
Here are young men with pushchairs, their giggling
Teenaged wives in wild mascara, tight denim,

And the imperturbable middle-aged
Looking in different directions.
The commentary has a neutral tone,
The history of torture like the history of art,

Periods, schools, the great virtuosi
Of the craft. The henbane Doctor Crippen used
Is a quiver of plastic leaves,
The Yorkshire Ripper wears a tuxedo.

At the exit sunlight slaps the face
And all the smirking children wander off
Into the fair. Behind us, in a darkened room,
The tracery of wax restores
A gleaming tear, the psychopathic grin.

The Attic

The ceiling shows the yellow stains
Where snow blew into the attic,
A paper-thin pale moss upon the beams
Wetting my hands as I swing
My weight in through the trap-door.

That frontier crossed, I take to trespassing.
The attic room a pelt of dark, the house's
Dreamless skull. I pause and listen,
Crouched sprinter-like over the boards.
And slowly there identify
The architecture of the drifts,
Their frozen combs of snow a yard high.

The torchbeam's dirty stripe of light
Lies brutal as a scar; no snow falls,
For these pillars have erupted
Like fungi, the midden in the middle
Of the floor a sheet draped on a chair.

In the room below my daughter fights
With sleep, her breath a handsaw's icy rasp;
Above, the aerial's hollow stem
Scraping its bracket. Panic has a metal taste.
Everywhere the mercury-coloured pools
Of settling snow lap against the joists,
And here beneath a broken slate
A drift of lilies grows taller by pale atoms.

I cannot touch this profligate:
The snow is furtive and obscene,
And when the wind rises the attic fills
With particles of light, a television
Screen that sucks me in. The blizzard
Is in the house, its voice like pigeons,
Such soft insistence on its mastery.

And I find I have always lived elsewhere,
That I have never known this place:
Old clothes and broken furniture, a bath
Of bulbs with tendrils black as candlewicks,
Sparkless but for snow. I breathe and hear
A breath returned, the flutter as
My daughter's voice thaws and freezes,
Freezes, thaws, and streetlight falls
Out of the roof like flakes of orange rust.

The drifts are grey and tiered like hives,
The swarming snowpoints hover and subside.
Ice on my clothes is fine as insect-wings.

The Looters

The helicopter cameras
Bring us the freeze frames.
A black sea outlines each peninsula
As snow finer than marble dust
Blurs the steeples of the spruce.
Bad weather, the wisdom goes,
Brings a community together.
Tonight the screen is a mirror
And the news is us.

At a house in Bedlinog
A drift has left its stain
Like a river in flood
Against the highest eaves.
There will be a plaque placed there soon
As if for some famous son,
While the cataract at Cwm Nash
Is a thirty foot long stalactite
Full of eyes and mouths
And the dazzling short circuits
Of a pillar of mercury.
An icicle uncirclable by three men.

Abandoned on the motorway
The container lorries are dislocated
Vertebrae. The freeze has broken
The back of our commerce
While on the farms, the snow-sieged
Estates, people return
To old technologies.

Meat is hung in double rows,
The carcasses identified
By the slashing beams.
Each one looms hugely,
Puzzling as a chrysalis
Under its silver condom of frost.
They sway like garments on a rack
When padlocks break and the freezer-
Doors swing out. It is too cold
Here to trail blood, where bread

Is frozen into breeze-blocks
And ten thousand tubes of lager
Sparkle under their ripping caul.
As flashlights zigzag up the wall
Tights turn red and tropical bronze
In each thin wallet.

The stranded drivers sleep in schools,
Their groups determined to uphold
The constitution of the snow.
Families smile through thermos-steam,
A child with her kitten, blue
As a cinder, sucking a blanket:
The usual cast of winter's news
As the commentary runs its snowplough
Through the annihilating white.

Outside the cars are scoops
Of cumulus, and toboggans
Polish gutters in the drifts.
We never see the looters.
They move somewhere in the darkness
Through the blizzard, beyond the thin
Bright crescent of the screen,
Those people who have understood the weather
And make tomorrow's news.

The Mansion

The house stands as it always has,
Its windows tall above the lake
And grass cut almost to the yellow root.

Along the drive a whitelimed kerb
Follows a perfect crescent,
As if stone, like air or water, moved in waves.

My steps dissolve in gardens where
The acid rhododendron thrives,
Its flowers pink and white as naked dolls.

It always was a selfish tree,
Devouring the light, growing
Glossy and alone, the strong inheritor.

At the door they take my card
And a name in silver italics
Grants entry where I never thought to pass.

These hands laid gently on my arm
Disturb an earlier trespasser,
That child under the yew hedge

Who watched the long cars slide through his village
And women shaped like candleflames
Moving over the lawns.

Above his head the berries swelled
As soft as wax around each nucleus,
The black nugget of poison that would grow.

In the Watchtower

The frontier hums, a live
Cable carrying our charge.
Barbed wire and the sentry posts
Bristle against a wall of acid firs:
Climbing the steps I'm brushing off
Their needles hooked into my clothes,
The needle wax's scent of oranges.

It's safe here in the clock-tower –
The villagers' dovecote –
Where sunlight varnishes the boards
And soldiers lean their guns
Against a wall, put down
Binoculars and take to twisting round,

Like farmers with a barren hen,
The necks of tall bottles.

And I smile as they step, dainty as girls,
Out of the rifles' harnesses,
Thinking of my grandfather
And the scornful way he'd leave his spade
After a morning's couch-cutting,
Relief flexing through the racked
Sinews, yellower than iris roots,
And spreading from the halfmoons of his sweat.

I've never seen a gun so close,
The grey snub-barrelled thing
Shining like a beetle's carapace,
No bigger than a toy's image.
But touching it might set the bells
Above us, now a cluster of blue grapes,
Speaking the first syllables
Of the last war, and loose the doves –
Preening on the shoulders of bellmetal –
In a volley over Czechoslovakia.

Those fields swim in a blue-green haze
Like the pages of a passport.
I stop, and feel the current stir
Beneath me, two armies praying
To the eager god of electricity,
While a family of leverets
Wild as pinball in the grass
Cross frontiers within sight but out of range.

Sunday Morning

I choose back lanes for the pace they will impose,
    An old perspective half-forgotten
Surprising me now as the world slows
With these things the broad road lacked:
    Carboys of vitriol stacked in a garage,
Orange hooks of honeysuckle gripping a wall.

Here a church window becomes an arch of light
   And the pitching of a hymn a slow
Infusion of the air. Voices, and low
Indistinguishable words, the organ's bass
   The foundation for a ritual
I trespass in, that suddenly

Intensifies the day. On the other side
   I picture them: the ranked devout
Pulling out the ribbons from the black prayerbooks
And each with his or her accustomed doubt
   Submitting to a poetry
Triumphant as the church's muscular brass.

Thus Sunday morning: a gleaning of
   Its strange wisdoms. The certainty
Of hymns comes with me through a different town
Of derelict courts and gardens, a stable
   Where a vizored man beats sparks from a wheel,
An old man splitting marble in a mason's yard,

The creamy splinters falling into my mind
   Like the heavy fragments of hymns,
Then walking on, much further, this morning being Sunday.

SHEENAGH PUGH

I chose these poems because I thought they came closest to saying what I wanted them to, and sounding as I hoped they would. Maybe some have personal importance too, but it's never that simple. 'A Matter of Scale' is about a friend who died in a motorbike accident, and it is sincerely meant, but it's true too that I loved the sound of the word 'Aldebaran' and enjoyed balancing the poem around it. And 'Paradise for the Children' concerns a danger which alarms me, but I also liked the technical challenge of playing with three different kinds of rhyme within each verse. I hope 'detached' doesn't equal 'callous', but I don't think poets can work effectively without being somewhat detached from their emotions.

Some poems can't help sounding serious, but I hate them to sound solemn or earnest. If you can treat a serious theme with some humour, as Aristophanes did war, I think it's all the more effective. I included 'Filing the Queen of Scots' for contrast, because it's more light-hearted than some. But there's a certain amount of humour, admittedly somewhat mordant, about 'Nothing Happened Here' and 'The Haggard and the Falconer'.

'147' is totally happy and light-hearted. A friendly review called it 'ironic', but I didn't mean it that way at all. Reviewers make assumptions. Three have told me I was influenced by 'the Movement'. For the record, before the first such mention I had never heard of the Movement, nor read any Movement poets. I read some later and didn't like them. The only poet I have ever tried to sound like is Robert Henryson, and he hadn't heard of the Movement either.

A Matter of Scale

He left no grief on Aldebaran;
Cygnus Alpha didn't know the difference
and the long lights of the Milky Way
never paled an instant for him.

Even on his own planet
the most people did not know him;
in his own country, his own town,
his loss was a small matter.

Only in a few lives
is a void left, wider
than a town could fill, or a planet,
or the great sun Aldebaran.

The Frozen Field

I saw a flat space
by a river: from the air
a jigsaw-piece. It is green
by times, and brown, and golden,
and white. When green, it gives food
to animals: when golden,
to men. Brown, it is ridged
and patterned, but when white,
a plane of evenness.

When frost touches it by night,
it turns silver: blue shadows
etch the hollows, grassblades glitter
in the grip of silence. It was
in such a place as this,
elsewhere, on the coldest night
of a cold winter, two boys
drove a car, with some difficulty,
over the frozen hummocks: parked
in the breathtaking chill, the stillness
that weighed each leaf down,
and shot each other.

It was a place I knew
years ago: I must have seen
the field, in summer maybe,
growing turnips, grazing cattle,
dotted with the white
of sheep, the blue and orange
of tents, and all the time
travelling toward one night
vast with misery; the sharp cracks,
one-two, like branches in frost,
that broke the silence.

Who knows what a field
has seen? Maldon sounds
of marsh birds, boats, the east wind.
The thin wail across the mudflats
is a heron or a gull, not Wulfmaer,
the boy who chose to die

with his king, never having guessed
how long dying could take.

And an oak lives
a long time, but a nail-hole
soon closes. Of all the oaks
at Clontarf, which is the one
where Ulf Hreda nailed one end
of a man's guts, and walked him
round and round the tree, unwinding
at every step?

The night the boys died,
their field was Maldon was Clontarf,
was Arbela, Sedgemoor, Solferino,
was every field where a moon
has risen on grass stiff
with blood, on silvered faces.
... Aughrim was so white,
they said, with young bones,
it would never need lime again:
better not to see
in the mind's eye Magenta,
that named a new dye.

It was as if the field
clenched all this in
on itself, hunched over
the pain of all young men
since time began; as if
every crop it ever bore
crowded in on it: barley, blood,
sheep, leisure, suicide,
sorrow, so much, its being
could not stay in bounds
but spilled out over space
and time, unwinding
meanings as it went.

They tangle around
the field's riddle now: *I saw a stage
for pain, a suffering-space.
The fine mist of aloneness closed it*

in the morning: at sunset
it was flooded with blood.

Thinking such things often,
we should see too much. I see
a picnic place, a playground.
My eyes half-open, I lean
against a tree; hear through the ground
children's feet chasing.
The sunlight shivers: *someone*
walked over my grave. I chew
on a stiff grassblade.

147

It's the magic number: seven more
than black despair, and that last black
has to be the hardest. He poises
his cue, and we all feel sick

with certainty: he won't make it.
That black is every job interview
we failed; every final step
we tripped on. It's every no

we heard when we needed to hear yes,
and it's going to happen again,
it's bound to.... There's the contact: too late now,
it's paused on the lip; we all breathe in,

and it's down, and everyone's going mad,
because destiny's taken a day off
and we've won. His laughter radiates
out at the audience; they mirror love

back to him, and everyone wants
to hold him, touch him, touch the luck,
in case it's catching. He did it
for all of us; he put down the black.

Torturers

So the grandmothers walk, softly, but their black
outlines are hard in the sun, to the big house
of the president, and they demand the children
of their dead children. In voices like ash,
white and brittle, they explain that the torturers
from the last regime, when they had quite finished
playing with someone, and put them away
for good, would not infrequently find
infants left over, and would take them
home to their wives: loot.

The president is a humane man,
and not a little intimidated, besides,
by the vast loss frozen in their faces,
and he says, certainly he will try to find
what's theirs. (To bring the torturers to account
is proving beyond him; where's the evidence,
the witnesses are dead, and anyway
he'd lose half the army....But to give back
the old women's grandchildren is justice,
for once, at a bargain price.)

So here and there, in a comfortable house
in the suburbs, some boy tries out
a new name on his tongue. The man
he has been calling father forced the screams
from his father; planted the electrodes
in his mother...And carried him home
to feed; play with. He tries saying: torturer,
but fails, because, when you come down to it,
torturers are human like any other men,
and this man loved him.

Paradise for the Children

This park's got everything. The floweréd fan
around the pool is a landscaped garden
that shades into woods. Paths shoulder
through holly thickets to the high field
edged with trees, a green shallow bowl
with a dark rim, and from there you see all
across the terraced streets, over to Leckwith Hill.

It's a world enclosed, from tame to wild
in little: *paradise for the children,*
but it's parents who occupy the ring
of benches round the formal pool, gazing
at the bronze eternal boy in a glitter
of light, elusive in the leaping water,
his calm classical face teasing the spectator

with the hard make of youth, the unkind
perfection. The children seeking and finding
in the bushes hanker for their freedom:
given the choice, they'd leave mum at home,
but she compromises; sits out of their way
by the fountain, hearing them nearby,
glimpsing them through the gaps of light in the dark holly.

A bronze butterfly rests on the boy's wrist:
the frailest thing on earth, and the hardest.
She listens for their voices: too long
without them, she grows restive. They're younger
than they think: cocky, trusting... That man
who was watching the ducks just now, alone,
where has he gone, and did he head in their direction?

Water splashing at the boy's feet,
he stands in a splintering of whiteness,
knee-deep in rainbows... *They didn't listen
when I told them stay together; where's that man?*
The sound of falling water, the planted scheme
of colour, is meant to leave the mind calm.
How are you supposed not to worry about them?

The man strolls back, authority in his step,
admonishes someone...he's a park-keeper.
She laughs at her fears, feeling, for an instant,
paranoid and foolish...But who says you can't
be an official, and a walking threat?
Teachers, priests, lawmakers have been that.
The naked boy poses on tiptoe, his bronze smile set

in mockery of Socrates and Plato
and all men whose wishes sink below
their words. *Did the sculptor's breath shake*
as he stroked your wax; indented your backbone
with his fingers? But you have been hardened
in the fire: no one can put a wound
on you now, so unchallengeably young as you stand,

and will always stand, year after year,
while the beautiful children of men grow older
or get used and thrown away, like some
whose mothers dropped their guard for a moment...
They wheel past, screaming like gulls; veer off
out of sight, shaking a peony's ruff
into a brief red shower, echoing the water's laugh.

Filing the Queen of Scots

The Queen of Scots
lamented much, in her captivity,
her billiard table, impounded
during her travels.

Her impassioned request
through official channels
about the *table de billard*
must have paid off, at last,

because her dead body
was wrapped for burial
in the green cloth.

The Queen of Scots
was unusually tall
and slender; she must have had
a good reach.

Long-fingered hands, the best
for making a bridge.

The historian notes her taste
for risk, her misspent youth,
tut-tuts; files her tidily
under 'queens: bad'.

But every act of filing
is a choice, and sometimes, in truth,
a cock-up: she just belongs
under 'billiards players: early'.

The Haggard and the Falconer

To make a hawk, he sits up and starves
with her; stays with her through the pangs,
the hooded blindness, the sleeplessness aching
in the bones: three days and nights. The effect,
oddly, is to bond them, as torturers
the world over could tell you. Afterwards
they're a team: she'll fly for him
and her own pleasure, wear his colours,
take food from his hand, save
her meat for him.
                         There are some, though,
that will not, and until she flies,
he has no way of knowing. A haggard
is a hawk that takes no partner
and shares nothing. Her keen eyes watch
her own chance; the dizzy vertical stoop
from the air, that catches the throat,
is for her, the kill her profit
and her delight.
                         So he sits,

light-headed, chilled with hunger,
watching her; awake wondering
what she is; whether he has her.
Some say a haggard is the fault
of the falconer, a want
of devotion; he mustn't fail her.
While she is making, he'll scarcely see
his wife: he went in briefly
two nights ago, before he started
the hawk. His wife, as usual,
lay unmoved, watching him
under her eyelids.

When he has gone, she gives
herself ecstasies, fetching, in the dark,
great raucous breaths, heart hammering,
bright-eyed, exhausted. She could show
him how, but she will not: her love life
needs no helpmate, and if you can fly
why share it?

Hello

All winter, no weather kept him in:
he'd perch his thin frame, right-angled
with arthritis, on an old chair
out front, in the scrap of waste garden
he couldn't dig. Whoever passed his door
ran the gauntlet of 'hello': not once,
but over and over, dogging them down the road,
as they quickened their pace; kept their distance.

However often the answer came,
it wouldn't be enough. It was as if
he were delaying the need to embark
on shipboard: as if the silent house behind him
were an ocean, and he standing in talk
on the quay, unwilling to leave behind
all the noise, the bustle, the harbour life,
and watch them slip out of sight and sound.

And now when the air has lost its bite,
and even in his garden, gold coins
of celandine gleam in the rank grass,
his door stays shut: has been shut
for days sliding into weeks. Unease
is starting to show now on the passers-by,
pausing, glancing at the drawn curtains.
If he is gone, nobody said goodbye.

InterCity Lullaby

They're both what, nineteen? Their dark hair
flops; they've had a long day on the beer
or the travel, sitting slumped in sleep,
each with his feet cradled in the other's lap.

Balulalow, beautiful tired boys,
and if I could, I would give you the choice
of where to spend your lives, and what to do;
you should not so be shuttled to and fro.

Newcastle United black and white
on their bags; they'll be in London tonight,
looking to find the streets paved with brass:
fairy tales are practical, nowadays.

Balow marras; balow canny lads,
and if I could, I would rebuild your trades
and let you play at home all seasons long
at doing what you liked, and being young.

Two stations back, they were talking about
the fair at Whitley Bay, while they ate
the food their mothers packed for them before
waving them off to look for their adventure.

Lullay innocents: lully, lully, lullay,
and if I could, I would make away
the witch: break spells, change the frog-prince's shape,
shut down the engine's noise to guard your sleep.

Nothing Happened Here

Nothing happened here.
There was no demonstration; there were never
young people singing in this square,
or if there were,

then they went home peacefully, filing out
at the army's discretion. Or if not,
then you could scarcely wonder at what
you say they got,

though they didn't. Nobody died,
except some soldiers in lightly defended
tanks, which were set upon, mob-handed,
by the misguided

counter-revolutionary anarchist
saboteurs (funded by the West
to ferment rebellion), who, as we stressed,
didn't exist.

OLIVER REYNOLDS

Though grateful to have been asked to contribute to this anthology, I feel rather shifty when it comes to taking responsibility for the choice of poems I have made. My first impulse, rather than commenting on the rather arbitrary reasons behind this choice, was to try and hide behind background notes to the poems. ('The statue in the fourth section was shown as a plaster cast at the Royal Academy in 1899 under the title *Joyance...*') A profusion of similar details may have provided some sort of protective colouring, but more interesting than the nature of such camouflage is the reason why it should be felt necessary in the first place.

It seems difficult nowadays for the poem to swagger into town and up the main street on its own; if it is seen at all, it will be limping self-consciously around the outskirts or stumping along after nightfall on a pair of critical crutches. The days of the Wild West are gone for ever. (The sonnet flashed in the sun as it was drawn from the holster. A poem's gotta do what a poem's gotta do.) There are few outlaws left and most of those have had haircuts. The feeling of dislocation is exacerbated when you have to deal with poems of your own. Silence would appear the most seemly resort; diffidence an awkward second-best; failing these, you can always give notes.

The titles of the first and second poems, written at a time when I was trying to learn Welsh, mean 'Countryside' and 'Geography'. The sixth poem is about Lewis Merthyr Colliery, closed down in the early 1980s. The city in 'Necropolis' is, at times, Cardiff.

Cefn Gwlad

Always like this:
The standing field,
The climbing cloud.
And between them,
Lashed or drifted,
The falling rain;
Nothing to do
But fall and fall.

The image fixed
Many years back:
Land, sky and rain.
In addition,
The men at work
On the humped hill;
Then with horses,
Now with tractors.

Always like this:
The trust in soil
And long slow work
With rain sealing
The unnoticed
Blurred horizons;
The standing field,
The climbing cloud.

Daearyddiaeth

The land was always worked.
It was what you lived on.
So the feelings were strong:
The land was in your heart;
The land was underfoot.

It's still farmed, flat and hill,
Some of it good, some bad.
Cash crops may oust *hiraeth*,
But it's still praised: *Gwlad, gwlad*
With the ball hanging air.

And many of the poems
Carry the smack of loam,
In books of earthy style
Whose pages you leaf through
Like someone turning soil.

It wasn't long before
Love and the land were one.
Sweethearts had their contours
While streams grew feminine.
Desire and greening joined.

The genre pullulated.
Venus came on vernal.
The body pastoral
Was sung or lamented
As was Arthur's, grass-graved.

What though of city loves?
Hamlet's country matters
Aren't foreign to the town:
We've enough to ensure
Cupid stays urban.

Poets of the precincts
Lacking parallels
Instinct with the instincts
Should exchange Arcady
For the brick of Cardiff.

Fingers that divagate
Along the vertebrae
Assume Sanquahar Street,
Sesquipedalian
Way to the timber yards.

The gasworks surplus burns
Behind Jonkers Terrace.
Wind flutes and twists the flame,
The gold column broken
Into plaits and tresses.

The path to Thornbury Close
Dwindles into Thornhill
Where tight dawn is seeping
Bit by bit into day:
Someone slowly waking.

At the side of the path
Is an old lamp-standard
Whose bulb is lit but pale
Above the base's stamped
And simple avowal:

D. Evans   Eagle Foundry
Llandaff   1911.

Parisien

I work in the municipal glade.
Today I have to coax the cuckoo,
Sharing my bread with him,
Possibly soaking it in milk.
At least my tobacco is safe.

I am happiest when I leave,
Looping the chain
Like metal vine
Through rusty gates
And clicking the lock.

I often pause then,
Hang my bag
(Holding a wine bottle and some crumbs)
On one of the railings
And take in the dusk.

Opposite the entrance,
Perched like flotsam above
The cobbled swell of the street,
Is a large wedge of apartments
Including my own.

In the half-light the building
Has a provisional look,
As if it were the memory of a film-still
Seen long ago outside a suburban cinema
Closed due to illness.

Theme and Variation

Ludwig had perfect pitch
and whistled wonderfully,
placing notes as easily
as putting a hat on a peg.

Paul, his pianist brother,
lost an arm in World War I.
Ravel wrote him a concerto –
the one for Left Hand.

*

You hear very little now
of Roger Whittaker.
Maybe he's concentrating
on a *Tractatus* of his own.

Nice if he still had
something up his sleeve,
like Nelson
after Tenerife.

Porter

The new incinerator is gas-fired.
Once, having left the burners on,
I returned to find the steel sides
glowing and throbbing.
Cooled to a flaky ash-white,
their hurt bulge is permanent.

It's mostly domestic rubbish:
paper, toast crusts, peel, boxes.
Aerosols crump in the fire's gut
or explode by the open flap,
slicing out metal into the air.

Occasionally, there are records:
lists of names, dates, conditions –
bare histories going up in smoke.
Some old reports are leather-bound
with sharp-edged endpapers
sheened in marble or porphyry.
Many are only half-full.
Pages clog, unburnt, in the flames;

when separated by the iron raker
they show white before catching.

The lab sawdust burns slowly,
often wet and sour with piss
and strewn with pellets of shit.
The rats are flung in on Wednesdays,
inert bumps in a sack
sharp with formaldehyde.

I once found a litter
burrowed in a bin of sawdust.
Thumb-sized, purple and blind,
they had soft tip-snouts
and kept cheeping thinly.

L.M.C. 1890

Crossing river, road and railway,
I pass the insistent notices:
'This bridge will be closed
if vandalism continues. NCB.'
Beyond the fence,
hundredweight chunks of motor
litter oil-caked earth
as if dropped during a robbery.

On this side of the valley
there are tables in the street,
flutters of bunting
and children eating and playing
to celebrate forty years
of Victory in Europe.
The kids play touch:
'On it. On it. Steve's on it.'

Dead ahead are the two wheels,
one stubborn with green paint
and the other rust-brown
with its cable running

uselessly tight
to the engine-house.
I remember the far wall
and the colliery initials
chiselled high up
above the opening date.
Five more years, I saw,
to another anniversary.

Walking back from Trehafod,
I found a small piece of coal
on the pavement
and it's now on my table:
an inch of memento,
a fossil's miniature strata
smattered with light.

I wonder if I'll still have it
in five years' time
and if I'll remember those kids
running down from the street
to the grassed-over tip
in their toy bowler hats:
plastic crowns brightly coloured
with slices of Union Jack.

Necropolis

Abraded and blinded
by a poisoned rain
the head of Minerva
on the library roof
has a consort of pigeons
Shit cakes the sky-lights
The single librarian
sleepwalking
shelves and shelves
of dust
picks at the scabs
of her nipples

The single reader
laughs noiselessly
blind head
thrown back
fingers flowing on
down the page

Listen to me
Listen to me
A sucker-mouth
breathing words
Listen
In out in out
a quick chain
of bubbles
only breaking
on the surface
only breaking
on your ears
Listen to me
Listen

The mirror factory's
brass band
is in full swing
in a room
lined with mirrors
The conductor's smile
tarnishes
as a saw
whines outside
Lopped cypresses crack
Trumpets quicken
Mirrors shimmer
The two bands race
first one ahead
then the other

The metal boy
thrusts
rigid arms
at the night sky
Is he tired and stretching
Is he wounded
At his feet
a duck potters blindly
in shallow water
Trees confer
Wind brushes
grass uphill
At the top
floodlights can be seen
across the city
Stars are lost
in the domed glare
and the moon fades
The wind sickens
with shouts

Because of the cuts
the school
hires out its fields
to a local stable
A boy watches
four whipped horses
gallop by
Torn grass and clods
arc up
and patter down
A handbell rings
in the playground
thinly
above drumming
hooves

Waves dun
at the sea-wall's base
Great heads of foam rear
dull white in the dark

Choose two pebbles
small and flat
Walk past the angler
with a storm-lamp
inside the calyx
of his umbrella
Slide through shingle
to the dark beyond
Lie down
Put the pebbles
on your eyes
Wait for the sea
to wash them off

Home

Beyond the striving tump of the ant-hill
and across the meadow thinking
of becoming marsh, you return at last

to this slew of timbers,
roof-beams grounded in grass
and, in the one wall still standing,

the door and its rusted padlock
that stood the test,
whatever test it was.

GRAHAM THOMAS

It is difficult to select from one's own work, and more so to explain why a particular poem appeals rather than another. In putting aside attempts to make any singular point, I have opted instead for poems that I simply like.

I do not know whether it is a consequence of my Welsh upbringing that the idea and the reality of belonging attract so much. It is not a question of ignoring the claims of the outside world, far from it, but home is where I am defined, made myself, and it is always there – just as, until now, the Welsh language has been secure in its heartland, allowing as 'Welsh' even those of us who have lost our mother-tongue.

'Border' belongs to a group of poems on the discovery that home was not inviolable. My house now stands alone, the remainder of the Row having been demolished. 'Wallace's Farm' and 'Bourneville' also refer to this continuing aspect of Valley life. There is an inevitability about progress which it is surely negative to resist, but I am continually drawn to the vacuum which seems to symbolize it.

In the earliest poem here, 'The One Place', there is a passing reference to the activities of *Mudiad Amddiffyn Cymru* in the 1960s. I could never condone acts which endanger life, but the sense of fear, of panic even, at the potential loss of something as precious as a Culture, did communicate itself to me then. T.E. Nicholas may have tramped the roads of Cardiganshire reciting his work, but at Ynysddu the poet Islwyn was no more than a name. In 'At Llyn Clywedog' I tried to reflect my own ambivalent attitudes, but with the important coda that there is a way back, if you seek it. Today, my family regularly visits North Pembrokeshire so that my son, who attends *Ysgol Gymraeg*, can better claim what is his.

'Papering in the Old House' is an epithalamium for my marriage. It is about a well-loved place, and the love to come. The other love poems, and those for my son, are obligatory, but I hope not too obvious. My wife is an artist in wool: hers is the scarf I saw between the trees alongside the dram road on Craig Ddu. Year after year I have watched them reveal themselves, layer by layer, exactly as the house did during its renewal. I should like to explore more layers, to go wider and deeper, but that is something for the future.

The House

Light slants in where the garden ends
And the room is nineteenth century –
Dark sideboard, hangings, portraits on the wall,
Front-parlour smell of must and damp –
And, in the centre, the oval table,
Half reflecting the cluttered shelf,
Half a brown and depthless sea.

I wanted to live where those others lived,
My family before me. Now, the house sleeps
Cocooned in its mist of paint and care,
And would not, had it a heart, demand
Such lengths, such time. But I've come to terms
With the mice that scurried above our heads,
With the groans in the floorboards and the last
Family of woodlice quietly churning
The skirtings to dust. All that remains
Enters my head on this autumn morning,
Or stays in the photo I took of the hearth –
Black brick and red brick, brittle with flames
Before we blocked it against the light.

Breakfasts

Each morning she comes down
Dressed for winter, summer and winter.
A cup of tea, a cigarette, and then
She reads aloud the parts of the paper
That catch her eye: a favourite story
With animals perhaps, or the weather, children;
Tales you would not care to read
Given the choice, or the paper, first;
And then the ritual of births and deaths
And the chance to tell us all, again,
How soon one comes after the other
In any, every house. We flinch
And scrape our feet under the table,
Crunch our cereal louder, make
Noises with the tea, but listen,
Unspeaking, till the end. Bad habits live
Long with us, and this one came
When she was a child – one of her tasks,
The first of the day, to read out loud
The morning paper to her father,
Blind at twenty-six, who never
Once saw his children but gave them all
A face, a name, choosing in her
His patient eye. And over the years,

Unable to spare the habit, she has
Kept alive the tie that grew
Between herself and him; passed on
To each new child who came to fill
His place around her table such
Moments of her joy, her fear,
They too, by listening, grew to see.

Papering in the Old House

Stripped from their walls, they become
Fragments of different patterns, colours,
And drift to the floor through the dusty air
Like boats unanchored, riding a storm,
The lime their medium. Each one
Becomes a remembrance, a harking back,
As room by room they are revealed,
Down to bare walls again.
                            Were these
Fountains of roses her consolation
When all her garden was ash? Or that
Geometry of lines and circles
A way of asking for peace, for order,
When there was none? The walls are spools
Winding the threads of language tight
With fear or laughter, love, hate,
The ebb and flow of voices caught
In stone forever. We imagine them
Stirring a little as the paper falls,
And we sweep the pieces into piles
Beginning, like the others, as we mean to go on.
We are the important spirits here,
In this place now. And they stand aside,
Warmed by our arrogance or our conceit,
But benevolent always, and kindly, kindly.

Border

The house is open ended now,
Bare stone exposed to the south, and the wind
Grating along it, turning there. All the time
It's raising slates from the roof, making
The rafters tick, the boards squeak drily –
A conversation that began
A hundred and fifty years ago
Between wind and wood and slate and stone
And still going on. More than anything,
That end reminds me of a castle wall –
Hard, rough-hewn, its strength in its thickness,
In another time or another place
Dividing kingdom from kingdom. But here
There is no border, nothing to say
Where one began, the other ended,
Or if they existed at all. Except
In the minds of those who stay and watch
The traffic and the people edging
Closer each day. The rubble of buildings
Surrounds them still, and the old ways
Are just as dead. Like the castle
Marooned in its sea of quiet green,
Bothered only by wind, by rain,
And, at its centre always, silence.

The Sweater

Christine, on her latest sweater, portrays
A pattern of lakes and rivers, mountains,
Two lambs at play in a grassy field
And, beneath a sky of blue,
A tiny house, a chimney smoking.

I do not know how my response
Is measured yet. But I am no traveller,
And landscapes such as this one, love,
Confuse, disorientate. Am I
Lost, perhaps, among the hills

On the journey home? Or, in my boat,
Stalled again between shore and shore,
Unable to reach you? And that house,
That house you built so carefully,
Was it I who lit the fire?

Two Love Poems

1

Once a week, then, it has
Become a kind of ritual.
You are the altar and the throne,
And me, the penitent approaching,
Always below your line of sight,
Always bearing gifts, surprises,
Like my voice, honed to a fine whisper
And, for my knees, two cushions.

2

I am the man under the water
Drifting just beneath the surface,
My presence undetectable
But for the stream of bubbles rising,
The spangles of light breaking the surface,
Betraying me there. I would stay this way,
Keeping in touch through a stalk, a reed,
Except that the water becomes your hair
And every way I breathe it is
You that I inhale, exhale.

Late Spring

Trees put on green
Suddenly, as though
Wakened with a start
From the dream of winter
By a blackbird singing.

We, too, arrive late,
Late and cold,
And bearing our doubts
Like gifts in our hands.

But the trees are the guests
At their own thanksgiving,
While we stand amazed,
Watching the canopies
Thrash in the wind,
Watching the change –
So quickly, quickly –
All arms and legs
Into such grace.

Tunnels

1

First, there is
The tunnel of spring,
Celandine and violet
On their vertical bank
And, high up, the boughs
Of the trees interlocking,
Lacing together
The roof of their church.

2

Summer comes there
And decorates, thickens,
Makes again
A greening cup
Under whose lip
The shadows bend
To an oval of light
Like the lens of an eye.

3

The tunnel of autumn
Is smoky, still;
Is a thousand colours,
Each one migrating
To the scarf of a girl
And all of its light
Filtering down
Through broken windows.

4

More light now
Than spring or summer.
Bare branches touch,
Completing the arch
Whose only procession
Is the wind, the leaves.
And freed, at last,
Of their burden of green,
They dance, dance.

Two Poems for Ieuan

1 Geography

You have come with your new geography
To test me out. The skin of your brow
Cradles the lost canals of Mars,
Is a maze of medieval fields,
Small hedges, tree-roots, contoured lines,
An atlas where I turn and turn
The pages endlessly.
                           Now you are watching me
With particular care. I am a spider
Upside-down on the ceiling, a colour
Flapping on the line outside. Do you
See me any way but this? Or am I
The landscape where you first discover
Lines of darkness as the valleys fold,
The cusp beneath the eye, a trace
Of darkness there? Bored with watching,
You turn to someone else, a different smile,
And offer your calm, unshadowed face.

2 A Pair of Blackbirds

Outside, in the garden, there's a pair of blackbirds
Doing the same as us. The slash mouths of their young
Gape at the lip of the nest redly,
Angrily demanding food. The parents provide.
We do as much, vying with them at dawn
As the baby bawls from his crib, and they
Panic as the beautiful predators
Come low through the grass.
                                        Should they survive,
They will pass on the song and the marvellous eye,
The note that soothes us and the warning call;
While Ieuan beams another smile
As I back into the dark, again,
Determined, at four o'clock, determined
Not to leave to him my dreams.

At Ynysddu

There were two surprises for us
On the road that day. First
The mill, the one I should have known
Because of the name Cwmfelinfach;
And then, as the road arched upward
Over the mass of the hill, the bluebells
Studding the hedges all the way down
Past Islwyn's house. Unexpected,
Finding them there, and commoner too
Than willow herb on banks, in ditches,
Beside the sudden stream, the school –
Heads of a vivid, spiky blue
That held us with their beauty, yet
Seemed alien for it somehow,
Out of place. I went expecting
The Big Tip and the shadowed streets,
The crumbling chapels with their high
Inscriptions hammered out in Welsh
All but forgotten. I saw them too.
But, driving to work each day, it was
The bluebells that I noticed, those
That come back every spring, the old
Promise to be true made good
Again and again. Turning my head,
I hoped to raise my eyes. Instead I saw
Only our own the alien now.

At Llyn Clywedog

You need to use imagination
To see it now as they did then.
Monuments soon revert to stones,
Deep reservoirs to sea-green pools,
And no man walking on the shore
Hears, far down, a tolling bell,
Or suspects it there. Today, a buzzard
Circled Pen y Gaer, its prey
Trapped somewhere between the icy

Water and the peak. We sat in the car
And watched it from the Viewing Point,
No more than ordinary tourists
Except for the time of year, the snow,
The picnic tables turned for once,
And our eyes, averted from the water.
Did we choose to come here, then,
To make amends? Because we must?
                                    Where we live,
Tryweryn, Clywedog, Claerwen, Fyrnwy,
Were never more than distant names.
Were never the sign they took them for:
Like lichen patterned on a rock,
The irredeemable stain. I have a liking
For moving water, not still like this,
And the image of those buttresses
Hollow, massive, 'like cathedral vaults',
I would not choose. For this is a place
You visit when the sun is shining,
Dispelling the eerie silence of it,
The flat and depthless calm. And best leave
Strictly by the road you came,
The one with No Exit painted on it.

5 Jan. 1984

Wallace's Farm

Wallace's farm lies under the tip
And the summer meadows – rocky, sodden,
Plagued with rushes – are his no longer.
The road slips by, sliding to the new
Contours of the land. And what remains
Stays in the mind more clearly now
The mountain crumbles, moves on. Like the beech
Cradling between its two forked halves
A ball of stone; or the orchids, their spikes
Awash in peaty water, tilting
Always as though surprised

By the immanence of traffic. And then, some mornings,
The shape of a man come out of the mist,
Returning home from dipping, from shearing,
His flock before him.

Bourneville

Two rows of eyeless houses lean
Across the valley floor to where
New tips supplant the old. Trees die,
Awash in unfamiliar shale.
Behind them, the mountain wears
Its brace of concrete like a ring,
Is wedded forever to the village
It would sooner destroy, but lived with now,
Ignored like the rain except for the shadow
Cast on the road on icy mornings,
Or the tick, tick of the white sticks
Impaled in its side like Chinese needles
We imagine as we're driving through.

The One Place

You can stay too long
In the one place. Year
Follows year and the same
Patterns are repeated:
You come to be contented
With them as they are, to learn
To love them for the way
They always stay the same.

But though they grow too close
For you to lose, you listen
Carefully as the land erupts
Outside their limits,

Half-hoping for a tremor
To reach as far as this, a door
Burst open and the shock
Of dissidence to welcome in.

Porthgain

Even the gorse lies down
Before such winds. Inched above the grass,
Above violet and thrift a yellowness
Like undiluted metal, outdazzling
The total blue of sky and sea
Enclosing us now. And what have we come
To collect this time? Speckled pebbles
For Ieuan, again, and purple fronds
Of seaweed for the rain, the vowels and consonants
As fuel for the fire which grows
With each new year. I look through the window
At the road untwisting in the village,
The houses turned from the sea above
A receding tide of boats and cradles,
Old lobster pots, discarded orange lines.
In the corner of the pane the water flicks
Greenly in its harbour. We will take a picture
Of that, and then another, something else
To ride with the pebbles and the shells
And the words he will learn to replace the old,
That feel more than home, and love, and wanting back.

CHRIS TORRANCE

I am a transplanted Celt. I was born in Edinburgh, Scotland in 1941. My mother was a Roman Catholic from County Down, Northern Ireland. My Presbyterian father was fiercely Scots in his loyalties, despite being born in Lewisham, London. I received an English education of sorts on the outskirts of London. In my teens churchgoing was replaced by jazz and bookishness. For seven years I was a legal executive in the City of London, West End, and Sutton, Surrey. Enthusiasm for the Beat writers led me to writing and eventually to becoming co-founder of *Origins Diversions*, an early 1960s little mag. I dropped out of the law to become a gardener. Under open skies I suddenly began writing with real freedom, and got published. I was sure of my vocation now – I wanted to be a poet. Influenced by Don Allen's anthology *The New American Poetry 1945-60*, my style was to be Open Field, which most suited my geographical, locational bent.

In 1970 I arrived in Wales to concentrate full-time on writing, coming to grips with my Celtic undercurrents, which up till then it hadn't occurred to me to question. The stones of Wales became my teachers, two in particular – Maen Llia at the head of the pass between Senni and Ystradvellte, silent, spiritual, bottomless well of consciousness both interior and cosmic; and Maen Madoc on the Roman Road, stern, bloody, admonishing yet encouraging. Together they have led me deep into prehistories, ice ages, evolution, Triads, Early Christian Saints, follies, herbs, dreams and wonders; and a little of the meaning of those great gyres, the waterfalls of the Neath Valley, possessing a magic so strong that it is easy to believe that this area is still the domain of Gwyn ap Nudd, King of the Fairies.

Alongside this Western Highland Zone re-education I have engaged in the writing of a continuous poem-series entitled *The Magic Door* which takes as its theme the transformation process in nature and in humankind. In my selection here I have tried to identify a few of the developmental threads that link the various books of *The Magic Door*.

I became a lecturer in Creative Writing for the Extra-Mural Department of the University College, Cardiff in 1976, where I have continued since. I had a modest hand in the emergence of the successful literary-performance group CABARET 246 in the mid-1980s, whose members mostly met for the first time in my class. Throughout my career I have considered performance to be an exercise central to getting the poetry all the way over to the audience, as an *enactment* of the experience or feeling of the poem. In recent years this has been occurring in the context of the poetry-&-music band *POETHEAT* in events ranging from rock and rap through to lyric and romance. In the 1990s I see my task as a combination of exploring the nature of the evolutionary puzzle in a book to be called 'The Ice Ages', and of continuing to develop *POETHEAT* as a vehicle versatile enough to stage anything I may write.

The House of Stone

The house of stone
stuck
like a worn & stubborn thumb
in the Glen of Mercury
buffeted by endless rainstorms

etched fabric of cross-birch,
cross-thorn & cross-alder
mimicked by miniature frets
of lichen outgrowths
encrusted on
dead twigs

swinging amongst catkins in the fork of a hazel
is the wind-stripped corpse of a dog fox
hindquarters bared by weeks of galewash
the naked balls hanging pathetic between
thighs holed by death-blow or carrion creature

Large drops falling from the black branches
mud & water thrown out from the welts
with every step taken

the floodgates of the loving season

February filldyke
February sproutkale
February pointbulb

Overgrown straggly hedgerows, through which
many holes & gaps have been worn by browsing stock

      the land drains slowly bogging up
        wormy mud for the woodcock
        & snipe up on the common; each quag
     releasing its abundance of soupy habitat for
    demoiselle, frog, pondskater, water beetle,
                rat-tailed maggot

crowfoot, water plantain & forget-me-not;
slippery green stones with caddises & tiny mussels
underneath

a wealth, a plethora, a foodchain

peregrine, takes the woodcock
fox, takes the woodcock
gun, takes the woodcock

his feathers & bones melt into the soil

St Valentine's Day

utter clarity
pressure rising
the land afloat
on love messages
six white wavelets
athwart the sky
thrilling tight vee
of six white birds
rowing strongly
from horizon to horizon
sun reflecting bright
from pale underwing
a rough grit conglomerate
sparkling with quartz pebbles
set into the matrix
barn owl flaps
over the burnt conifers
denizen of the cartroom
at Glan Yr Afon
stone gothic folly
whose vibrations
prick Mena's skin
she had said to me
in the New Inn
amid the rattling crash

of stentorian conversation
Dai roaring over his pint
his face aglow
today brings his gun
& hounds & terriers
to the burrows
to hunt fox
as I drift down to the river
to pick up
water-rolled & bruised
orange shale, & long arm
of storm-wrenched damp ash
to be brought back & dried
small birds bobbing
through bare branches of alder
insoucient haze
drapes down over the South-Western basin
while aimless stratus casts
sharp blue shadows
onto the hills
the fire-tower conning
blindly, uselessly

The Fox

I am
Brychan,
the Red-Haired,
of Garth Madryn

I am a fox
I retire
to a lair
Other foxes

live by me
in their burrows
their dens
their lairs

I like
my burrow
I like
to have cover

I
am Brychan, foxy,
light of foot,
maybe a little
short of stature

I am a knight
seeking folly
bearing a dictionary
not a lance
into the wilderness,
a place
of no boundaries,
of no law
of no MAAT
faster than light
slower than time

a love saxophone peeling
a near-empty dancehall
a few shadowy couples
circling
or lounging at
corner tables

the fox
under linen
eyes bright
silver dowsing fork
glinting in jaw
trotting out over
shiny parquet flooring

pulling on the rope
over the wall

I am the fox
pulling you through changes.

'Resolving to set the Brychan monolith upright'

Resolving
      to set the
            Brychan monolith
        U
        P
        R
        I
        G
        H
        T

I have made a heap
        of discovered things

4th/5th century AD –
        famine, plague & pestilence
        affect proto-Brecknock

Marchella, daughter of Tewdrig of Garth Madryn
to Ireland, with 300 retainers, to seek a husband

²/₃rds of her force
        perish of the cold
            on the way over

Marchella brings back as consort
Amlach, son of Coronach, a king of Ireland

of the union
        of Marchella & Amlach
            is born BRYCHAN
eponymous founder of a dynasty
        that lasts 500 years; half a millenium!
'It takes not sloth
        to found a dynasty'

The kingdom of Brycheiniog survives
                an almost Egyptian length of non-history time
        for there is no direct history of this time
                        a legion of legends
                        a few inscribed stones

At an early age, Brychan was sent into fosterage with the king
of neighbouring Powys, as was the custom of those times; & the
young prince came under the tutelage of the soothsayer Dricchan,
'. . . who, although then blind, saw a vision on the riverbank, at
the confluence of the Honddu with the Usk, of a wild boar; & in
the water behind the boar there was a stag, & under the stag
swam a fish. A beech tree grew on the riverbank, & in the tree
bees had made a honeycomb . . .'

the vision   foretelling, presumably
                                    that the fruits of the land
                                    would be under Brychan's
                                                governaunce

Later, Brychan, by persistent legend, has some 24 daughters
& 16 sons, both in & out of marriage, numbers varying in
different manuscripts

Many of these daughters & sons become early Christian
saints, founding in the 5th century AD many llannau or
monastic settlements which are often strategically
placed for the defence of the borders of Brycheiniog

Stones were set up by the wayside
        in the Roman fashion
& specifically on the military road network
        that stayed in use until medieval times

certainly Llia, the feminine lozenge,
        wide-hipped, ponderous, earth-wise
        is more of an enigma
than the redbrown, fiery, upright
        pillar of Dervacus, son of Justus
        bedded in the causeway, Sarn Helen

1500 years a vibrant node
       accumulating wind & water power
       sun power, earth power
       resistance slowing down the sphere
dug up by
       modern archaeologists who affirmed
       a large square cistvaen
       but no human remains
       in the acid humus

The Celtic Church cut off from Rome 150 years
on the Western fringes of the dissociating empire
the seas controlled by barbarians & pirates
yet hermetic ideas filtered up from the Med
the roadside stones parallelled
                     in North Africa
the early Christianity a patina
      warped & woofed upon
        the more ancient palimpsest of druidism

A Further Canto for Brychan

.   .   .   he   early   having had issue
                                Cynog
                       out of wedlock
                         from Benadlinet
                     a princess of the
                     House of Powys
                     wherein he was fostered

.   .   .   a hot lord was he & unlettered
             that knew to correct his own faults

.   .   .   but Brychan stored grain against famine
& rode the federation territories
         kept peace on the frontiers
         'easy to start a war, less
         easy to finish one'
– brought calm in vine climate
                 breasthills of the kingdom

. . . rents & forfeitures were abolished
'you can't rook people who have so little'
– gained their co-operation instead

& consulted the wise women of the parishes
              those splendid pictesses, Cymry, co-proprietors,
speckled folk of stones & trackways
              herb women, washers at the ford
the old laws memorised, coded in dry doggerel
the Christian precepts gradually absorbed & adapted
an overlay grafted onto custom & usage
                    legend & season-stone

. . . each princeling or chieftain
              leading his kindred
                    to baptism
         – druids sons to monasteries
              daughters to nunneries

mashing, planing, & smoothing
                    the onion bed
a pig's tusk, shards
                    of a coarse red pottery surfacing
I am at the
         blind point of history discharging

Lunar   tides
move in our   blood
gently knead   the mass of earth
can be measured in a tea-
                    cup
the woman-tide
         moving in men & women alike
causing
         continents to ripple

the Neath Disturbance
         birthed in the basement rocks
Caledonian

        fault lines growing through
newly-accumulated sediments,
                the
shearing, the
'calcite-riddled thrust-zone'
in the fault at Craig - y - Dinas

den   din   Dinas
'The Rock
       of the City'
midden   mixen   vixen

Cities of ant barrows
        populating strategic ground
the wriggling of
        tree branches into the sky
the earth's
        coiled ball of energies
the orange shale pavement
        an interstitial in the Grit series
        I consult the leaning maen
        at the crossroads, holed
        top & bottom   perhaps
        a very old railway sleeper
             definitely
        a sleeper

the capsule upended in the earth

the eternal poem in motion through time

attuned to the curve of the zodiac.

JOHN POWELL WARD

I have had a kind of theory for some years now but it would be hard to elucidate it. I have always felt a contradictory pressure; the wish to write a very clean and simple poetry, and the compulsion to fore-ground language, as sentences or words but also as letters. (The latter drew me toward the concrete poetry movement of the 1960s). In both cases I like the result to be transparent, so that a linguistic object like a piece of glass or snow results. It should be a visual object, like print itself. In both cases I draw, to some extent, on the Welsh (in English) metaphysical tradition, as I find myself calling it, with Traherne, Hopkins and others as admired influences. Robert Frost and Wallace Stevens (probably because of my time in Canada) and Wordsworth, Dylan Thomas, Herbert and early R.S. Thomas also rang true for what I wanted. If only one could emulate them.

I don't think the poem's topic should be too explicit or direct. Outstanding poems are certainly written on clear issues like nationalism, race or gender, but it occurs when the topic is not just 'subject' but the poem's matter, the actual medium it is made of, just as a painter uses paint. To me the sudden huge consciousness of the environment in recent years seemed pennies from heaven, but when I try to write a poem on an environment-pollution story which makes me angry it isn't often successful.

I think that poetry is a way of projecting light through language in the same way that, increasingly, we now see TV art programmes enhancing great paintings. It makes them translucent. One ends up then, certainly, seeing the 'subject' of the poem in a fresh way, but it is because the language itself gets exposed, turned face up to the light, and the subject itself glows surprisingly and unexpectedly. Unexpectedly to the poet too, who doesn't even know what he/she has written. The poet is a blind seer.

So this selection of mine is the poems I think most get toward what I have tried to describe in these remarks. The occasions of most of them were wholly unpredictable.

Bristol Channel

(*Meditation and water are wedded for ever.* – Melville)

Or any coast...Miles out a white
Wave rolls in the distance like a whale's
Belly showing. A single tip
Of white vanishes like a far ship
Going down. There are nicks and falls
Of white so far out at sea they seem
No more than notion or idea of foam,
A nail-paring. A pale hand seems to wave
Then fade, like a riding-lamp seems to give

One beam then not be, a lace
Curtain's corner falls back into place.

Another wave's a sheet laundering.
One like a bar extends its length
And not alone. Through binoculars
Its folding follower jumps in close.
Seen nakedly, small again, but coming.
The next seems like the first's new try.
I'd look for ever, as out there an eye
Does at me, each wave making
New sense, breaking yet not exactly breaking
And soothing the weak sand's brow because
Wave's work is rough as no man's is.

Men once thought it was horses out there
Or a voice singing. You could say so.
Now I cognize a watery shape
Of horse as made by Proteus' deep
And primal as any white-tipped mare.
Beyond, Homer's highway of fishy fins
Up and down channel in sixteen lanes
Permits such legend, cutting across
The tide's direction, drilling its course,
Sending wave on wave in just to you,
Thinker. It comes in just for you.

Evening Bathers

A creamy warm Atlantic thins
And washes up the cockles. Where
The August sun goes down and near
A nervous mother tiny boys
Adore the swirlings round their knees;
Stick-insects, laughing skeletons.

A surfer leans his thighs to guide
The pink foam to a beaching-place.
A girl stares at the fishing-rod

Wedged in the sand. Bent from a catch
The curling tendril makes a snatch
At air. Before a rock's blue face

Last families are cricketing,
Ball sailing like a red-beaked gull
To be caught. The sea's rolled shavings steel
Themselves to come on in. Along
The hedgerow of each blossoming wave
The surfer rides, we divers dive

Under the saline drift for words
Down in a luminous green weed.
Philologies crash overhead
Above our continental shelf
And waist-deep fathers stare amazed
At orange and the sky itself

To see come catapulting in
The surfer's black cat like a seal.
The evening bathers feel so real
In their mauve caravans tonight.
They watch the huge tomato sun
Drop bouncing on its trampoline.

Incident after Walking

She was just thinking the bus would
never come, in that leafy-green
village pouring with rain in the summer, when
he went down the steps of his terraced
cottage. She was soaked but didn't call out.
He smiled, even though they were both so wet.
      He asked her if she'd like
a cup of tea and to dry off a bit. It was
obvious; she'd have to stay a while, have
a bath while her blouse and stockings dried.
      When he went up the passage
he stopped at the door, hoping the water
was hot enough. 'It's OK' she called,

not seeming to think about it. 'You can come
in, I don't mind.' And he could have gone in,
so gentle and even. But he hesitated and went
to the spare bedroom to find a jersey.

      She lay there
so warm and heard a noise in the passage.
Of course; he'd need his towel from
the bathroom – after all, he'd got wet too.
There'd been none in the kitchen, only
a brass hook on the sill with some screws
to be screwed. It made her think
of the absent towel and even
saucepans. 'It's OK' she called,
not seeming to think about. 'You can come
in, I don't mind.' She stared through the steam
at the wooden-planked door, as his step
faded on the carpet. She felt exposed
and small. Could he ever now respect her?
Rain was still falling, the sun now
edging out from clouds with grey facings.

Apple Incest

I climbed the apple tree today to touch
The tart, stiff, acid, red-green fruit we've had
In each October of our lives. Our sad
Proud father straddled twenty feet and much
Too riskily took basins, sacks and such
To pick them in. But when an apple's bad
We throw it now across the lane to thud
Into the churchyard wall, and from the crutch
Where branches split and where the ladder leans
We shake, and hear good apples drop to turf.
That fall of apples, oh so sensuous.
I felt my sister's apples, this thing means
That bark-grazed mossy branch we've spoken of
Was formative, bending the shape of love.

At the Pool

We stood there on a winter day.
The rootless horn-wort always seen
In shallow moorland ponds was there,
This pond a spring and watering-hole
For Gower horses. Picked, this weed
Had dangling a tube of slime
Meniscus on the emerald green.
Immersed again it spread its full
Feathers about in loose relief
Back in wild, icy water. If

We looked at it, we stared at it
In fact, just like a 'nature class'
Which we in some ways have become,
Living out here. Bogweed, starwort,
A long-haired not a spongy moss
We'd never seen, its thrilling stems
The legs of centipedes. And this
Was all so tiny. Aren't we so?
Our own three faces loomed above
The oasis in the gorse and thorn.

Sun's cold December face looked down
By ours and found the beetles there.
A thousand of them under ice,
An exhibition under glass.
Tom picked a handful of the mud,
A leggy water-louse was pulled
From weeks of sleep and came to air,
Knowing its moment suddenly.
It nudged and nozed the ooze till Tom
Lowered it gently back, like I

Would settle him down into bed
At night again, when woken up.
Every jump that insect made
Had human feeling, human verb.
You pressed a hand down on the ice.
A bubble slid beneath across
Like mercury, sword-blades of grass
Sent shadows to the greasy floor

In globules, several beetles moved.
Whirligigs, Tom's brother said.

Such winter, and no sound at all.
Where have the creatures gone, their shells?
The tiny decomposing wings
Of damsel-flies? No trace or sign.
Above, a hunter jet alone
Then two, one miles away, its sound
Pursuing like an open jaw
To swallow men up, like a pike.
What do these microscopic things,
These wee crustaceans know? How can

We say we aren't as them? Our whole
Galactic night a molecule
On some aquatic being's leg
Or hair. I cling to the belief
In something more than human life,
A trillion times ourselves or else
So small no microscope could see
Its skin. A bird clicks, rattles in
The thorn bush, scrapes the air, its throat
A castanet and zips away;

Off from its island in this pool
Worn by the horses come to drink
Who slice the clay away, each mound
An island. Lines of algae fill
Canadian pondweed's swollen buds.
Our careful faces leave the bugs
Their biosphere and stronger spring,
A bubble underneath each wing
For buoyancy. We walk, blow frost
And God knows what else round the sky.

Still Life

And he purchased, a very large green
bottle, of yellow wine, and he took it home, and
he put it on the sideboard, while he cooked veal
with sauté potatoes, and celery, and laid the
table, for himself, and a second place, and he
walked back to the sideboard, and picked up
the silver-plated corkscrew, glinting in the
evening light of the yellow sun, which was
splintering the window's glass, and he held
the bottleneck in his fist, its bottom, and punt
away from him, like a thrusting knife, and he
put the corkscrew's point at exactly the
centre, of the cork's texture, and he pushed
and turned at once, with his palm's heel,
pressing on the handles, and saw candlelight
in the bottle's green glass, and he
pressed, so that the circling spiral, went
into the cork, and then he held the dark green
bottle, contrasting his white hands as it did,
away from him, but with the palm upright, and
held the corkscrew, and pulled very hard, and
there was a satisfying deep noise, and he
sluiced a little wine, into a glass's
transparency, and held it up, by the stem, between
thumb and finger, like a flower, and tasted
it, and put the bottle on the table, so that
its green, and the yellow wine, and the bowl
of green apples and grapes, were together, and
there was a tap at the door, and he straightened
the mat, at the second place he had laid.

London Welsh v. Bridgend

Then I got on the train, very late
at night, Saturday, and lay on the seat,
exhausted, as did the other man
there, a little man, beady-eyed and
with a pointed chin, and he pulled the

blinds down, and we lay, and just about
dozed off when bam! door opened,
in came half a rugby team, enormous
fellows, tipped me off the seat on the
filthy floor, then sat down, singing,
shouting, crashing on each other with
their beer cans, and one sat by the
beady man, running his fingers exquisitely
along the fellow's thigh-bone, through
his trousers, but in only a bawdy
way, friendly even, if you could believe
it, and they roughed, and one
arse in the corridor undid the fire
extinguisher, soaked us, and another
slammed the door, sat down again, kept
asking me the beady man's name, which
I didn't know, angry now, afraid even,
but decided to be sensible, and got
going, talked, had their beer, and they
got serious to meet me, a most
generous gesture, and a big man, older
than the others, kept deflecting the
attention, of the bawdy one from the
beady one, the bawdy one trying to make
the beady one talk, which he couldn't,
in inhibition, and cringing fear, and I
felt sorry, but leant on the carriage arm,
with them, drinking, singing, yawning, and
hearing about his wife, from one of them,
till, at last, they were quieter, they had
won their match, they had had a good day,
and they dozed off, one on my shoulder, sixteen
stone, snoring loudly, but I finally dozed
off, at the train's rhythm, rattling
through the darkness, and I half-woke,
at times, saw a misty scene, as of Arthur's
knights, assembled, swaying, brief white
faces, then dozed, felt the train stop
in my half-asleep condition, and men get
out, a shrieking porter, and banging doors,
then slept again, and then woke, two
hundred miles from London, they had
all gone, every one, bar the beady one, and I

sat, heavy, soggy, wanting lukewarm tea, and
saw, with my round eye and my mind's eye,
the aftermath of dawn, and the mess of the
twentieth century; the industry, the steel
works and the smelting works, a new day, for
better or worse in our hands, and the
carriage window, filthy, but a filter,
for that streaky, watery, nearly
light-blue, blue.

The A40 Wolvercote Roundabout at Oxford

'O' the ubiquitous, the wheel.
A while if only for a while.
A lawn reflecting orange light.
A helipad whence to depart.

Why is he restless? Moons about,
Disturbs the static April night?
O the ubiquitous prayer-wheel,
The ring of lamp-posts tapering tall.

'Welcome to Scholars' Oxenford'
And watch the town roulette-wheel speed
Its bits of centrifugal thought
Off at all angles to the night

As cars brake to its edge, then yield
To let a prior group roar ahead
Then move themselves, or tucked behind
Swing to an exit out beyond,

An arc of concentrated thought.
He paced a little, sensed them do it,
Sat on a civic bench to watch
Them merge and hesitate, guess which

Split-second move a car would make
So miss some other overtake
Some other. None of them remained
More than an instant in his mind,

Not knowing what each driver bore
Most deeply, fears, obsessions, for
Those shed, like clothes, they dropped away
For one lone vagrant passer-by

Witnessing all their stop-start game.
He only saw them go and come
Lane-dodging, weaving, and the wheel
Their curvings made contain them all

As persons, work to suck them in
To this spun centre with its own
Illuminata, then away
To 'Stratford, The North', infinity

Lucy

The word is light.
Then switched on, 'light'.

Sunlight is LIGHT.
Stained glass gives LxIeGwHaT.

Hidden light is (light).
Humour is ?light?

Jewels sparkle l*i*g*h*t.
Joy flashes: light!

Bowls of fruit are light.
Boy twins are light.

Light on your dear face,
Like that, is sheer grace.

Up there on his Horse

The holly with its brilliant berries of blood.
The footprint lying in the centuries' snow.

Des Dolan sits up there on his horse
Downing punch at the Boxing Day meet in the morning.

He is Master of the Hounds in his red coat.
Hegel looked up at Napoleon once

Like that, numbed at the arsenal of power
Locked on one saddle, out in the agora.

Once he nearly played rugby for Ireland.
Only the selectors determined otherwise.

Ants suffer, and mice do, and petrels, and fish.
And all God's creatures in their kind.

Word Work

Badly I need you, you, and that
Body you gave me when I gave myself.

Windows are where you always stand,
Wondering if even summer rain is heaven.

Live as us both, whenever die,
Love still recedes and won't be named.

Sing like you did, but just for me,
Songs we recall, but not the day.

Are we? Is? The question and alone
Air making ready all you have become.

NIGEL WELLS

The selection is based upon the criteria that each of my three published titles be represented, that any attitude common to them be reflected and that I do not in the foreseeable future, expect to be ashamed of, or embarrassed by their use of language.

'Introduction' from *The Winter Festivals*, particularly the third and fourth lines of the penultimate and final stanzas, make some attempt at summarising what propels the majority of my poems into being.

'Dydd Gwyl Eneidiau' and 'St Cecilia in Sagittarius' from the title sequence reflect my own pleasure in folk-song, street-rhyme and liturgy.

I've always had an affection for 'Morben Isaf' not only for the memory it invokes but the fact that arising, as it does, from a relatable incident it is easier to introduce at readings than most of my stuff.

'Bulkington' is one of six figures in the sequence 'Wilderness' each of whom represents in some way a character facet of singer/writer Jim Morrison who died in 1971. The two brief appearances of Bulkington in Melville's *Moby Dick* suggest to me he is the antithesis of Donne's 'no man is an island', a pure and dreadful example of utter self-sufficiency. Aloud the piece works quite well with a second voice reading the parts in parenthesis.

The centuries of both complex and simple worship practised in, and accumulated by, old churches can make them feel like virtual power-houses. Concerned with the compatibility of faith and doubt, 'The Porch' is one of several poems to have their beginning in such a building and to follow this theme.

I enjoy working within a structure so a group of near-sonnets was a satisfying exercise. The titles 'The Stone Woman' and 'That fence over there' are two of five given to students at a creative writing course I taught on – it seemed only right that at some time I produce my own efforts.

'The Six Points' came about more because of their seductiveness as poem titles than from a desire to comment upon these points of Christian ritual. I have chosen 'Vestments' and 'Incense' from the group because they are short and highly charged – qualities I like and respond to in others' poetry.

Salman Rushdie speaks of art replacing religion in mediating between the secular and spiritual world. For myself it serves rather to enhance and to qualify.

Introduction

he has not but the one red eye
to blink the sandy works of the sun
                                        – Anthony Conran

I see a water eye
Whose water eye is that?
I touch a throat
That throat is cut

An old religion put
Some muscle on the back
Now prayer is offered
But the spine stays slack

The eye minds not
That throat's slow leak
Nor heeds one bit
The tongue's dry squeak

Those blind apostles knew
With nerve and spit they died
Such seeing as they had
Divides and subdivides

And still that wet eye swims
While film builds on its mote
An irritant believer sounds
One high and edgy note

Will ever once that eye
Go shiver into shards?
I am this pepper speck
That smarting eye regards

Dydd Gŵyl Eneidiau

Bara can Bara can come to the door
Give to the feast of the dead
An apple a cherry a plum if it's red
Purchase a prayer from the poor

Bara can Bara can barley meal bread
For the dear and departed a sol
For the knitter of stocking the mender of shoe
For the childer at home in the bed

Bara can Bara can come to the door
Give to the feast of the dead
Salty cake or smithereened head
Souls going past on a cart

St Cecilia in Sagittarius

Three weeks into the waterdog month
Sun grows thin in the gleam
Sweet Cecilia of sightlessness
Gentle our path
Sister of tongues tell the way

For a mist off the moon clouds the glimmer
The bowmaster dims in his shine
Oh lady of visible musicks
Easy us under the arrowing stars
Sweet sister of song shape our day

Morben Isaf

Will skin sing
Shot blasted under rain
Or poor flesh swerve
In the path of storm

A questioning of form

I sing myself
Cadaver's musical,
With bodily accompaniment
Put airs upon this grace

There's no sense
To this wind
I lean
To the estuaries

To where

Fleeced again
Old axe backed ewe
Is in the bracken and
A world away

A fine pair
Her with her wreck of lamb
Me with my knee on fire

I quote the body song
As fault develops
And the swart blood pinks

It's queer here
All God and robbery
And booming in the ear

My scrag tune lilts
To the wind's pitch
What mends
In the wind's pinch?

I sing

Not only beauty shines
The lame
Have brilliance too
And dully gleam

Bulkington

1

The live part (here)
     is (largely)
     irrelevant

     what awes (should) is
(in the case of *one Bulkington*)
     the gathered force
     or soul.

2

Being little though (us)
The body bears
some small import
please (we say)

     Skinny minds.
     He was (will ever be)
     like this

A spine
     to match masts
A heart
     made water-tight
Complexion
     a hull's darkness
Teeth
     sea-ivory, white

AND

the eyes
(so long submerged)
surfacing
blood-filled (enough)
to float small joys
all memory.

3

Could any share
(five miles down on the water stair)
that shape, that tongue?
Would any dare (on the bottom rung)?

Consider (Ishmael, Ahab) peeping
eyes and the heart far down and
hoping to rise and needing to drown.
Consider (is it the tale we chase, is
it the tail?) that weed-green crew and
mostly (his desolate hue) the Whale.

4

Of the ship, the sea
and the maskless man

remark only
        that he took the ship to sea

mark him
        (in watery air)
        both diver and climber

remark
        he took the ship to sea.

5

It comes back to
boils down to
(blubber is blubber you know)
the soul
      (that crowded isolate)

      for
      where our giant goes we (should)
      (on a tide of sea-blood) go
      and (not ingloriously) see
      how

demigod
(without creed, without prayer)
by his own law

      sails
      from the soft hazards seawards
      voiceless
      to the brink of fear.

The Porch

St Tydecho, Mallwyd

Porches were considered as outside the church, and penitents
who were not allowed inside the building could do penance and
receive absolution there.   R.R. Sellman, *English Churches*

*The porch...over which is suspended a prehistoric animal's
rib and patella, dug up below the church about one hundred
and fifty years ago.*

1

Prodigy and providence?
A dead giant and a dying one?
Metaphoric turns?
The Word quite bare of flesh?

The fact of bone demands excess.
The fact of faith – pure doubt.

So it is
the doubt of fact
recalls us to the fact of doubt
which fact
remakes us as the fact of bone.

Our recourse
faith (again)
or gush (marrowslain)
more blood, more verse.

2

Any special moment, special find:
a chained gate to a keeling porch
for instance (by a lilting tower);
jackdaws in the usual (knowing) yews and
something collapsed across a shining perch
strengthening by the hour.

This particularly might bind
one who might approach
the wood-pile (it grey as grave-stale flour)
but might not hope to find
an entrance to (might not even search
for) such squalor and such power.

3

Old monsters crouch
in sham or awkward fight

and bruise with darkness
bruise for light

not real malice
not true spite

but 'fearful symmetry'
that first delight.

These monsters clinch
embrace, take flight

then boneless in the air
unite.

The Stone Woman

These endless versions in the well-known guise,
many in bas relief upon a corbel frieze,
some free-standing, bird-slimed under trees
but ever, seemingly, without the use of eyes.
Lady, do you know me by my gross remarks
(my great uncouthness is appearance for your sake)
and lady, know if what I knowing take
is got for plunder, or is struck for spark?
I itch to know you, but an effigy
in hard core, however finely wrought, attracts no trust;
whom I ache for's live – or living dust,
these rocky dollies only muddle me.
This day, to random, unsexed stones I'll pray.
Whose idea of woman are you anyway?

'That fence over there'

That fence over there; because it fenced nothing,
being ridiculously damaged, and
because a long term patient had, with grand
design, tagged each knot and jag of paling
with a tissue twist, a packet scrap – graphic lints
for what soft wounds? Also, the hospital wall;
because it signalled how the desperate call;

'pterodactyl pills' wrote one communicant,
another chalked his voice 'bloody feet on
iron roads', another put just 'please'. Such
works and words are things to which I lurch
but, Christ deceased, what drags ecstatic moan
from you – are these hard pulsings of the heart
(decoded or enshrined) to you just art?

Vestments

I suspect there is
somewhere the stillest
lake and it is surely
bound by hills of purest
black and oh so lonely
– were you there you'd
know about alone – and
there a huge nude bird
like scaffolding
careened in lappy water
freezing mud and oh so
seared – this toppled
tower has clearly felt
the whitest fire – well
were you there 'damn
pile of stalks' you'd
bluster 'is it crashing
in or crawling out?' and
at a chill lit in your
throat turn the collar
of your feather coat.

Incense

The smell of pleading
though corrupt
does not offend God's sense

That pleading smell

> a fleshed voice
> flakey with decay

> a plaguesong
> drifting off the skin

God relishes

breathing its rank fire

> my mother's burning bones
> these half-cremated cries

PENNY WINDSOR

I chose 'Dancing Woman', 'Like Oranges' and 'Heroines' because these poems share with the reader a woman's secret world – dancing naked at night, drinking wine in bed all day, dreaming romantic, heroic dreams. (Also 'Heroines' comveys a strong sense of the town where I live – Swansea.)

'Swimming for Pleasure' and the love poem 'I had imagined' celebrate women's sexuality and sensuality.

'No Bonking in the Corridors', 'Mothercare (Spain)' and 'Stag Party' – the stories of a disastrous teenage disco, looking after a baby in difficult circumstances, and a stag party in a Swansea pub – are included as examples of experiences many people have shared, told in a straightforward but humorous way.

'The Preparation' celebrates a woman's power to defy with laughter the intrusion of man's technology, and 'Kings and Queens' salutes the power of the goddess who is also queen and mother. Both poems deal with politics in its wider, more fundamental sense.

I have included 'Watch the Skies' because its an uncompromising, tremendously energetic poem – readers are commanded to watch the changing skies in peril of their lives.

And I have chosen 'Celebration' because I always use this poem to end my poetry readings – it is simple and effective, and seems an appropriate 'finale' to a collection of woman-poems.

Dancing Woman

by day
I go to work
and cook and shop and sew and mop
say the proper thing in the proper place
with a pretty smiling face
have three children and a spouse
a keep fit class, two library tickets and a mortgage on the house

but late at night
and out of sight
I throw my clothes away
and dance

at night
I am a clever witch
a scheming bitch
a madonna sick of sainthood
a mother tired of being so good
a princess who will not go to sleep

a widow who declares she will not weep
a school girl who says she will not be a wife
an independent woman with her own exciting life

at night
I might be anyone
at night
and out of sight
I throw my clothes away
discard my children and my spouse
my keep fit class, my library tickets and the mortgage on the house
and dance

quite by luck or chance

no one has guessed
the secret I confess to you
yet walking down the street
hair neat, make up discrete
I sometimes tap the paving stone
skip between the cracks
unwittingly betray the fact
at night
and out of sight
I throw my clothes away
and dance.

Swimming for Pleasure

I make love with the sea
arms and legs wide open
waiting for the next wave
the sun shining on my breasts
my toes curled up with pleasure

you would be jealous if you knew

like oranges

i am a no-good
waster-of-a-woman
drinking wine in bed
hair unkempt
face crinkled up
with sleep and sex

i dream away the days
watching
the sun steal unswept rugs
catching
dots of dust

basking

the sun seduces me
my breasts are sweet and ripe
and i am full of juice
like oranges

oh-
i am a lovely
wanton
wicked
wayward
waster-of-a-woman

I Had Imagined
(for Tony)

I had imagined
a soft summer sun
a lazy late-day heat
and a delicious delicate sadness
floating among the curling leaves
as the seasons turned

I had imagined
the lake lapping near our feet
the faraway sounds of children
the slight movement of trees

I had imagined
we put our books aside
and I lay back on the tickling grass
with the sun on my face on my legs
and I had imagined me full of honey
and you
sweet and heavy inside me

I had imagined
we lay undisturbed –
and the sun slipped in the lake
and a chill sheltered in the forest air

I had imagined all this
as each summer passed
with no comment condemnation celebration
I had imagined
that never again
could this happen to me.

Heroines

We are the terraced women
piled row upon row on the sagging, slipping
    hillsides of our lives
We tug reluctant children up slanting streets
the push chair wheels wedging in the ruts
breathless and bad tempered we shift the Tesco
    carrier bags from hand to hand
and stop to watch the town.

the hill tops creep away like children playing games

our other children shriek against the school yard rails
'there's Mandy's mum, John's mum, Dave's mum,
    Kate's mum, Ceri's mother, Tracey's mummy'
we wave with hands scarred by groceries and too
    much washing up
catching echoes as we pass of old wild games

after lunch, more bread and butter, tea
we dress in blue and white and pink and white
    checked overalls
and do the house and scrub the porch and
    sweep the street
and clean all the little terraces
up and down and up and down and up and down the hill

later, before the end-of-school bell rings
all the babies are asleep
Mandy's mum joins Ceri's mum across the street
running to avoid the rain
and Dave's mum and John's mum – the others too –
    stop for tea
and briefly we are wild women
girls with secrets, travellers, engineers,
    courtesans, and stars of fiction, films
plotting our escape like jail birds
terraced, tescoed prisoners rising from the
    household dust
like heroines.

Stag Party

they are magnificent
caught in a brief quickly-passing moment
beer bellies lurching gently
over motherly-pressed trousers
carefully cultivated whiskers
pruned and pampered
in early morning rituals

a herd of hunting men
caught in the strip light

they are the stags
struggling with seasonal horniness
coming out
in all their brief glory
a breath-taking moment –
the last urban wild life
red-faced and beer-brave
cruelly tortured
the ball and chain on their noble feet
breadwinner brands tattooed on their marvellous chests

tomorrow they will be part
of our past
now is our last chance
to put them down –
on tape and video
those strange semi-detached creatures
struggling for survival
in the back waters
of a stagnant Swansea swamp.

No Bonking in the Corridors

We were the bouncers, see
at this disco
actually we were friends –
a fifteenth birthday party
a friend of a friend –
to be frank
I was the mother

Disaster –
we did the right things
hired a hall
ghetto blasters
made food, watered the punch
threw out the drunks.

And the rules
well, they were clearly stated
'no puking, no fighting
no bonking in the corridors'

Well, I can say now
there was no fighting
the police came once
blaring and screeching
took away four boys
for stone throwing –
but, no fighting

Puking – well. I'm afraid there was
oceans of it
young men under threat
swished it round with mops
and smiled uneasily
retching became reassuring –
they hadn't died in our care

we became skilled with buckets
strategically placed
the light-on, records-off, police-are-coming, tactics
the hall emptied – except for the hopelessly drunk
the dog ate the biscuits and nuts

I prised a couple apart
lifting the tiny young man through the open door
while the heavily-breathing girl
cried 'I love you, Gary'
puking over the floor

Much later
the girl fell off her chair
and hummed
and a lad full of punch
thought he was Rambo or Rocky V
we cleared up his illusions

Well, as mother bouncer
I can say
I will laugh, given time
like several years, decades maybe

and I can say
thanks to the other bouncers
a colleague, a neighbour, a friend of a friend

there may well have been drunkenness
and limited debauchery
and certainly with drink and sick, the place was – well –
honking
but there was absolutely
absolutely
no bonking in the corridors.

Mothercare (Spain)

I would give three awards
and only three –
one to the maker of wet wipes
two to the maker of disposables
and three to Fundador
brandy cheap and rough
great comforter
for those involved with shit and wind
on nights without a moon
in faraway places
where no tourist that I know has ever been

The Preparation

she was completely still
in the pool
mountains on each of her hands
sunshine on the soles of her feet
the valley cupped below her head

so when the jet plane
struck
swinging across her
staining the lovely cross she had made
crucifying
she was prepared

she drew the pool tightly around her
held the mountains firm
fastened the sun to her feet
the valley to her head –

and laughed

Kings and Queens

'I am King'
he said
'my god is King of all he rules
and he rules all
and, I, a lesser but important King
rule over wife and family
stern and firm and fair
    these
        I care for
        earn for
        fight for
        and would die for'

'I am Queen'
she said
'and Goddess
I am the child I was
the mother that I am
the old wise woman that I hope to be

'King, you say that you would
                    care for
                    earn for
                    fight for
                    and would die for
              wife and family
              that your god rules all
I say to you
foolish and mistaken man
              you must
                    give your love for
                    lose your god for
                    recreate yourself for
me

'For I am Queen'
she said
'and Goddess
I am regal in my stride
I have magic in my eyes
and I hold the world of gods and kings
warm and powerful between my thighs'

Watch the Skies

watch the skies
they are changing
the clouds are massing
black along the coast
winds are gusting from the west
there are long shadows
sea like mud
and towns as dark as night

watch the skies
they are on the move
earthbound
and eyes cast down
you have already missed

the storms
and may well miss the sun
blazing through the thunderclouds
smashing the horizons
transforming black skies into light

watch the skies
they are changing
look up and read the signs
you may
even now
be just in time
to see the days turned into night
to witness frontiers falling
stormed by galaxies of light
if not –
earthbound
and eyes cast down –
you might as well

be dead

Celebration

with broad shoulders
we carry food and coal
with strong legs
we keep moving on
with powerful arms
we reach to the sky
with tough hands
we mould our lives

and through wide hips
our daughters are born

Acknowledgements

Acknowledgements are due to the following magazines, publishers and institutions:

For the poems by Bryan Aspden, *The Anglo-Welsh Review*, *Planet*, *Poetry Wales* and Seren Books.

For the poems by John Barnie, *Critical Quarterly*, *The New Welsh Review*, *Poetry Wales*, Mariscat, Dangeroo and Headland.

For the poems by Duncan Bush, *Ambit*, *Poetry Review*, *Poetry Wales*, *Southern Review*, BBC Radio 3, BBC Radio 4, the Welsh Arts Council, Seren Books, Hutchinson and Bedrock Press.

For the poems by Gillian Clarke, Carcanet Press.

For the poems by Tony Curtis, Seren Books.

For the poems by John Davies, Seren Books.

For the poems by Christine Evans, *The Anglo-Welsh Review*, *Poetry Wales* and Seren Books.

For the poems by Peter Finch, *Bread Loaf Quarterly*, the Welsh Union of Writers, *Poetry Wales* and Seren Books.

For the poems by Catherine Fisher, *The New Welsh Review*, *Western Mail* and Seren Books.

For the poems by Steve Griffiths, Rex Collings and Seren Books.

For the poems by Paul Groves, the Arvon Foundation, *Encounter*, *Orbis*, *Oxford Poetry*, *Poetry Wales*, *Quarto*, *Times Literary Supplement* and *Wayfarers*.

For the poems by Douglas Houston, *Bête Noire*, *Planet* and Bloodaxe Books.

For the poems by Mike Jenkins, Seren Books.

For the poems by Nigel Jenkins, *The Anglo-Welsh Review*, *Planet*, Galloping Dog Press, Gomer Press and Seren Books.

For the poems by Huw Jones, *The New Welsh Review*, *Planet*, *Poetry Wales*, *Radical Wales* and Gomer Press.

For the poems by Stephen Knight, *The Honest Ulsterman*, *London Review of Books*, *London Magazine*, *New Statesman*, *Times Literary Supplement*, *Western Mail*, BBC Radio 3, Faber and the Welsh Academy.

For the poems by Hilary Llewellyn-Williams, *The New Welsh Review*, *Planet*, *Poetry Wales*, *Other Poetry*, Seren Books and the Poetry Book Society.

For the poems by Christopher Meredith, Seren Books.

For the poems by Robert Minhinnick, Christopher Davies and Seren Books.

For the poems by Sheenagh Pugh, *The New Welsh Review*, *Snooker Scene*, *Western Mail*, the Poetry Society and Seren Books.

For the poems by Oliver Reynolds, *London Magazine* and Faber.

For the poems by Graham Thomas, *The Anglo-Welsh Review*, *Poetry Wales* and Seren Books.

For the poems by Chris Torrance, Albion Village Press and Galloping Dog Press.

For the poems by John Powell Ward, *The Anglo-Welsh Review*, *English*, *New Poetry*, *Other Poetry*, *Planet*, *The New Welsh Review*, *Poetry Durham*, *Poetry Wales*, *Poetry Nation Review*, *The Rialto*, BBC Radio 3 and Seren Books.

For the poems by Nigel Wells, Bloodaxe Books.

For the poems by Penny Windsor, *Momentum*, *The New Statesman*, *First Time*, *Spare Rib*, *Poetry Wales*, The Women's Press, Lovebards Press and Honno.

The Editor and Publishers are grateful to the poets for permission to reproduce their work.